BOUQUET OF GOOD-BYES

Carole Gift Page

MOODY PRESS
CHICAGO

To my friend Kasey Bryant
of Mesquite, Texas,
who also has a heart
for God and music

ISBN: 0-8024-8180-9

1 3 5 7 9 10 8 6 4 2

Printed in the United States of America

1

Where do you think we'll be in five years?" Kasey Carlone tossed out the question in a ho-hum manner, but she didn't feel ho-hum about the subject. She really, truly wanted an answer.

But her boyfriend, Ryan Dimarco, looked at her with the kind of exasperation he reserved for terminally dumb questions. "What do you mean, where will we be? Like, will we still be on this planet in this solar system in five years? Or will humanity still exist in five years? Or do you mean will we still be sitting here at this Pizza Hut in Springfield in five years?"

Kasey picked at the crust on her slice of double cheese pepperoni. She hadn't planned on getting philosophical in the middle of a Saturday afternoon, but the question just sort of popped out.

"I mean, what do you think we'll be doing five years from now?" she said, feeling a little irritated that Ryan had answered her question with a question.

He shrugged, clamming up suddenly. "I dunno. Haven't thought much about it, Kase."

She eyed him impatiently. Ryan had the dark, chisled features of Emilio Estevez and the zany charm of Kirk Cameron. But at times he could be a pain in the neck. Like now.

"You must have thought about it. Everyone thinks about the future sometime."

"Sure. Me too. Sometimes." He bit into a wedge of pizza and pulled it back so that a string of cheese hung suspended from his lips. He sucked it up like a snake zapping up its prey. "But, to me, the future is next Tuesday, or next month, or next summer, not five years from now."

"But don't you ever wonder what your life will be like—what career you'll have, whether you'll be married and have kids—?"

"Right now all I can think about is getting through high school graduation in June."

Kasey broke off another slice of pizza and nibbled at the pepperoni. "And all I can think about is college next fall," she said wistfully.

Ryan nodded. "I know. You're still bummed out about not going to Juilliard, aren't you?"

Kasey felt a lump in her throat. Yes, Juilliard was still painful to talk about, but suddenly, at Ryan's prompting, the words just spilled out. "You know I've dreamed of studying at Juilliard's School of Music since second grade. My piano teacher studied there. She told me I had the talent to make it there too. I grew up assuming that was my destiny. Juilliard. A successful career as a concert pianist." She twisted a strand of cheese around her finger. "But now I know it was all just a child's impossible dream, like growing up to be president, or a superstar, or first lady. It'll never happen."

"You don't know that. It could still work out. You passed the regional audition in Chicago in February. You could still be accepted."

"Right. But what good would it do? I still don't have the money for room, board, and tuition, Ryan. It costs a mint to live in New York City."

He nodded. "Too bad that scholarship didn't come through."

"And too bad my dad's still out of work," she added ruefully. She pushed her pizza aside. Suddenly she wasn't hungry anymore. "It's been over four months, and he still hasn't found a job. I don't dare even mention Juilliard around him anymore, because it makes him feel so bad. He feels like he let me down."

Ryan gave her a penetrating glance. "Is that how you feel too?"

She flinched. "I try not to. I know it's not his fault. But when he was working, he promised to help me with my college expenses. And now—oh, Ryan, he may need *my* help with *his* expenses!"

Ryan picked at the remaining crumbs on the pizza platter. "It's tight around my house too. My dad's paycheck doesn't cut it, and my mom can't work with four little kids still at home. I try to help out with my part-time job at the Kroger Store, but being a box boy at minimum wage, it's the pits."

Kasey chewed thoughtfully on her lower lip. "It beats cleaning houses like my mom's doing. I help her sometimes when I'm not in school or practicing piano, but I'd much rather give piano lessons to the neighborhood kids."

"The trouble is we're both still working for peanuts," said Ryan. "I keep thinking there has to be some way to make things better. But there's no way I can get a good paying job without an education—and that's going to take time. Lots of time."

Kasey nodded. "For sure. I try not to complain, but it's hard. You know, Ryan, when our gospel team went to Mexico City last Christmas and we saw all the poverty and heartache, I felt so thankful for my life here at home. I didn't think I'd ever feel ungrateful again."

"Same here," said Ryan. "That was a real mind-blowing experience. I'll never forget it."

"But I can already feel myself slipping back into my old attitudes, and I hate it. I don't want to feel impatient and bummed out. But it's like my life is going in slow motion and I want to hurry it up. I don't want to keep spinning my wheels. I want to get on with what I'm going to do in life."

"I feel that way too." Ryan reached across the table for her hand. "I feel that way about you, about us. I feel like our relationship is on hold. Sometimes I even think we're growing apart, heading in different directions. And that scares me."

"It scares me too. But how can we keep it from happening?"

"There's one way. We'll still be together if you stay here in Springfield and go to junior college with me."

Kasey sat back and pulled her hand away. "You know I'll be here. I have to go to J.C. I have no other choice."

"But I know it's not what you want. I just wish you were happier about staying here."

She slowly met his gaze. "It's not that I'm unhappy about being with you, Ryan. I love being with you. But I can't become a concert pianist here in Springfield."

He nodded. "I know. I can't become a doctor here either. But I can get a couple of years of college under my belt and save for the big time."

"It'll take megabucks for medical school."

"Right. So maybe I'll do something else."

"Like?"

"Like be a fireman like my granddad. Or a teacher. Or maybe even a missionary in Mexico. I got really stoked helping Pastor José in Mexico City. And it was cool witnessing to that Mexican street gang and seeing some of those guys come to Christ."

"Yo! That was totally cool! But I didn't know you were thinking—you mean you might really give up becoming a doctor?"

Ryan brushed his hand through his thick, wavy brown hair. "I dunno, Kase. Everything in my life is still up for grabs. All I know is I get a charge out of working with people, whether it's poor families in Mexico City or the elderly people at Shady Oaks. I like helping them and making their lives better."

Kasey smiled. "That's what I love about you. No other guy I know gets excited about helping people."

He looked at his watch. "Talk about helping people, we'd better head out to Shady Oaks. We gotta be there by six." He fished in his pocket for his wallet and tossed some change on the table.

Kasey grabbed up her purse. "Is everything ready for the program tonight?"

"Far as I know. Your brother and I got everything set up last night at the community center."

Kasey slipped out of the booth, and they walked hand in hand out of the restaurant.

"Imagine! My big brother actually helping out. Will miracles never cease?"

"Don't knock it, Kase. Keith's been different since we got back from Mexico. The trip changed him like it changed us all."

"For the better, for sure. But Keith's still a dweeb. He calls me 'Goggles,' even though I wear contacts now. And 'Slimeface' when he's totally burned."

Ryan opened the car door for Kasey. "That's a brother for you. You oughta hear what I call my sisters when I'm steamed."

"I have. 'Dinosaur breath,' 'Picklepuss,' 'Mooseface' . . ."

Ryan laughed. "OK, I confess. I'm not my sisters' favorite guy."

"Yes, you are," she said, slipping into the passenger seat. "Your sisters are crazy about you."

"Tell them that." He shut her door and walked around to his side and got in. He stuck the key in the ignition, then reached over and drew Kasey into his arms. "We won't be alone for the rest of the evening, Kase," he said softly, "so we'd better grab a kiss while we can." He kissed her lightly on the lips, then came back for another kiss, and another.

Finally, Kasey pulled back, catching her breath. "Ryan, if we don't get going, we'll be here all night."

"Sounds like a plan to me," he murmured, nuzzling her unruly mane of wheat-brown, sun-streaked hair. "You're beautiful, Kase."

When Ryan said that, she always felt warm and happy inside, even though she knew it wasn't true. She had stubborn tresses the color of cornbread and molasses and pale eyes that were robin's-egg blue. She had a face so ordinary she sometimes had to look in the mirror to recall her features. But when Ryan said she was beautiful, she knew it was so, if only in her heart and only in his eyes.

"We'll have some time together later tonight," she said as he started the engine. "When you take me home."

"Yeah, sure. If your folks aren't up." He pulled out of the parking lot and merged with the sluggish late afternoon traffic. "Or if Keith's not watching the late show. Really, it bugs me sometimes. There's no place we can go to be alone." He looked over earnestly at her. "And I'm not saying I wanna try anything. You know that. I'd just like to spend some time alone together."

"Me too," said Kasey. "But your house is always bursting its seams with people, and there's always someone at my house, with Dad not working and my mom's odd work hours. And, of course, Keith always pops up like Houdini, when you least expect to see him."

"That's what I mean. It's like we can only snatch bits and pieces of each other's lives. We're always tied up with other people, always on the run. Our time alone—it's never enough."

"Maybe someday—" she began. But no, there was no use talking about someday, not when the future was still so uncertain.

Ryan must have picked up her vibes because he said, "Someday may never come, Kasey. Maybe all we have is now."

She looked at him. "Is that what you really think?"

He shrugged. "I don't know what God wants for us. Who knows? Maybe He wants us on opposite sides of the globe."

"Like Outer Mongolia and Timbuktu?" she teased.

Ryan didn't smile. "Actually, I don't know what you want for us either."

She was silent for a minute, then said in a small voice, "I don't know either, Ryan. I just know I want to be with you."

"Always?"

"Always."

He turned onto the street heading for Shady Oaks. "So back to tonight. Do you think we can spend some time at your place without your folks or brother breathing down our necks?"

Kasey chuckled. "I think so. Keith has a date with Laury Lassen tonight."

Ryan whistled. "Well, knowing Laury, it'll be a late date."

"That's what I figured. Keith thinks she's a total babe." Kasey paused, then ventured, "Of course, that's what you used to think too, right?"

Ryan grinned. "For sure. Laury's totally fresh."

Kasey bristled. "Ryan Dimarco, how dare you!"

He elbowed her playfully. "Come on. I'm just kidding. You know Laury and I are only friends."

"That's not how she tells it. You're 'just friends' like—like—"

"Like you and Dusty?"

Kasey's voice rose a decibel. "Give me a break, Ryan! Dusty and I are—"

"I know. Just friends. In your eyes. But not in his."

"That's not fair. I have to be nice to Dusty. He's my grandparents' hired man. He's practically one of the family."

"Yeah, I think he'd like to be one of the family. He's had the hots for you since the day you met him on your grandparents' farm."

Kasey folded her arms defiantly. "Ryan, my grandparents' farm is in Middleton, hours away from here. I hardly ever see Dusty."

"No, but you write him. And he writes you."

Kasey shook her head in exasperation. "You are usually the most reasonable boy I know—except when it comes to Dusty. Then you totally freak out. When are you ever going to get over your insane jealousy?"

"When you stop being jealous over Laury."

"I'm not jealous."

"Me neither."

Ryan pulled into the driveway of the Shady Oaks Retirement Home and parked in their usual spot. Kasey gazed at the old Victorian mansion with its arched windows, steep roof, and sprawling front porch. It stood against the darkening sky with a solemn dignity, nestled between two towering, gnarled oaks with drooping limbs. The ancient house was weathered and worn but somehow ageless, like its brave, stalwart residents. Kasey loved this place, even if it did look like Disney's Haunted Mansion or something out of an Edgar Allen Poe novel.

She looked over at Ryan as he turned off the engine. "I'm sorry. I guess I lost it. Can we back up and be friends again?"

"Sure. More than friends," he said, giving her a quick hug. "I love you, Kase."

"Same here."

He blew her a kiss, then opened the door. "Come on. We'd better get inside. We've got a big evening ahead."

2

Clarisa Huckabey, a matronly woman in a white uniform, greeted Kasey and Ryan at the door with an expansive smile. "You're just in time. We're all ready to go. Your friends Selena and Jenny have already left with a full car, and I'll be driving the van. If you could take Mrs. Smolin, Mr. Suttles, and Mrs. Pinkelman with you, we'll be all set."

"Sure," said Ryan. "I'll help them out to the car. What about their instruments and costumes?"

"Everything's in the van," said Clarisa.

Kasey was glad that the community center was just a ten minute drive from Shady Oaks, so that her elderly friends wouldn't tire before the program. Every month the Shady Oaks residents put on a musical or variety show at the community center to earn money for the retirement home. So far they had purchased a big-screen TV, a VCR, and a stereo system. Now they were saving for their own Camcorder.

Kasey looked around at her gray-haired friends in the backseat. "So are you all ready to perform?" she asked as Ryan pulled into the parking lot minutes later.

"Indeed, we are," said Mrs. Pinkelman, adjusting her flowered hat on her halo of silver-white hair. She was a pillow-shaped lady with a generous nose and twinkling hazel eyes. She claimed to have sung in vaudeville with George Burns before he met Gracie. She could still belt out a song with the best of them. "I'm singing 'Some Enchanted Evening,'" she told Kasey proudly. "I sang it off Broadway in *South Pacific*, you know."

"I love it when you sing that song," said Kasey.

Mrs. Pinkelman smiled, a hint of nostalgia in her eyes. "Well, Mary Martin did it better, but I held my own with her. Dear Mary was at her best with 'Gonna Wash That Man Right Outta My Hair.' You should have heard her on that one!"

Ryan got out and helped Mrs. Smolin out. A squat lady with a big smile, she had once been President Roosevelt's cleaning lady. She could regale audiences with her whimsical tales of the White House.

Kasey escorted Mr. Suttles and Mrs. Pinkelman inside and down the hall to the small room backstage where Kasey's best friend, Selena Hubbard, was already helping people into their costumes.

"Hey, Kasey, you're right on time," said Selena in her usual husky, booming voice. Selena was a brassy, big-boned girl who had a way of making her presence known wherever she was. She had lost more than twenty pounds since last year, but she still had a way of seeming "bigger than life."

"Everything going like clockwork, I hope?" said Kasey.

"For sure," said Selena. "Jenny's with the signing choir, going through their number. The Venerable Skewbald Band is setting up on stage. And Olive Solomon's in the powder room. She said she wants to see you before the program."

"Any problem?"

Selena shrugged. "She didn't say. But that lady's pretty closemouthed around me. Around all of us, in fact. Except you. You're her pet. She'll talk to you."

Kasey found Olive Solomon in the powder room sitting at the makeup table staring into the mirror. She was dressed in a long, black, '30s-style gown that gave a measure of grace to her bent, stubby body. Her crepe paper cheeks were smudged with rouge, and her pencil-thin lips were lined in red. She wore her wreath of gray hair like a crown. Her expression was somber until she looked up and met Kasey's gaze.

"Ah, my little one, you are here at last," she said, turning slowly in her chair. "Come. Sit down. Talk to me."

"Are you OK, Mrs. Solomon?" asked Kasey, pulling a makeup stool over beside her.

"Yes, I am fine, child. But I look in this mirror and I think I am too old to sing. The mirror shows an old woman ready to die. I am a fool to go onstage and pretend to entertain an audience."

Kasey reached out and put her hand over Olive's. "That's not true, Mrs. Solomon. Your voice is still strong and beautiful. People love to hear you sing. I love to hear you."

Olive smiled wistfully. "You are a dear child. And you have helped me come a long way since we met last year. Because of you, I am no longer a solitary person, a recluse. But at moments like this I realize I am no longer the celebrated opera singer who sang for royalty. And I admit, it saddens me."

"Maybe you don't sing for royalty anymore," said Kasey, "but when you sing you make people feel like royalty."

Olive patted Kasey's cheek. "See? You always know what to say. You make an old woman happy. I wish my Sol were still alive to meet you. He would agree. If we had a granddaughter we would want her to be like you."

"You are like a grandmother to me, Mrs. Solomon," said Kasey with a rush of emotion. "You're one of my favorite people in the whole world."

"Ha! To most people I am a brittle, bitter old lady."

"No, not anymore. Not since you've begun to sing again."

Olive's dark eyes glistened, and the pockets of flesh under her eyes deepened. "I am not a pretty person inside. The anger is still there. The rage lingers like a mushroom cloud that has nowhere to go. For all of these years I have never talked about this to a living soul. Except you, Kasey. You listen to me like nobody else does." She paused, as if debating whether or not to go on. Finally, in a wavering voice, she said, "I have told you this before, and now I tell you again. The horror of the death camps stays with me, here inside me, always. Always. It is like a cancer that eats away my soul."

"I'm sorry," said Kasey, her gaze moving inevitably to the awful Nazi tattoo on Olive's inner forearm. "If only you could forget. The Holocaust—it's been so many years . . ."

"But for me it is like yesterday. The memories are born anew every morning. The sounds, the smells, even the acrid taste in my mouth. What happened fifty years ago is more real to me than what happened last week or last month. Can you understand that, Kasey?"

"I—I guess so."

"No, you are too young. You still look ahead to life. You are just beginning. Your face is open and untouched and innocent. I pray to God you never experience what I experienced at your age."

Kasey nodded thoughtfully. "I get all caught up worrying about exams and college and my music. I can't imagine being afraid for my life or seeing my family taken away and killed . . ."

Olive's voice grew raspy and hushed. "We were packed into boxcars like cattle. I thought the train ride would last forever. We could not sit or move, only stand. If one had to use the toilet, he had to do it where he stood. I thought I would suffocate or be crushed. Finally, when we arrived at the camp, I saw green grass and open space. And I thought, *This will be better than the train*.

"But then they came—the men in uniforms—and tore me from my parents' arms. My father was a big, strong man who never showed emotion, but I saw tears in his eyes. And my mother screamed when they dragged my younger sisters from her. I never heard my mother scream before. And I have never stopped hearing her scream since that day."

A lump of emotion swelled in Kasey's throat. She blinked rapidly, fighting back tears. It would never do for her to break down in front of Olive Solomon. If Olive could contain such horror without weeping, surely Kasey could control herself.

"And you never saw your family again?" Kasey asked.

"No," said Olive solemnly. "My parents were stripped and taken with many others into a big building. The guards told us it was the delousing showers. Many went in. But no one came out. We knew it was a house of death because the stink of death filled the air. The smell of burned flesh never went away."

"Are you sure your brothers and sisters were killed too?"

"Of course. I never saw them again. I was at the camp for many months, and I never saw them. If they were still alive, where were they? Where are they now?"

Kasey nodded. She couldn't think of anything else to say. It was all too horrible, too incomprehensible for words. She looked up at the clock. "It's almost time for the program to begin. Will you be able to sing tonight, Mrs. Solomon?"

The elderly woman smiled with her eyes. "Yes, Kasey. With your kindness you have helped me find a song again. I will sing for you."

3

After the program at the community center, Ryan drove Kasey home. It was after 11:00 P.M. when he pulled into her driveway.

"That was some show tonight, huh?" he said, slipping his arm around her shoulder. "Those old-timers were in rare form."

"It was totally fresh," said Kasey. "The band was up, the signing choir was super, and Mrs. Solomon was terrific as usual—"

"You weren't so bad yourself," said Ryan.

"Well, I have to admit, playing for an audience is a lot easier this year than last year."

"I guess experience is the key, huh?"

"And seeing the expressions on the people's faces when I play."

"The audience was the largest we've ever had," said Ryan.

"Sure. The word is spreading. Shady Oaks puts on

great entertainment." She paused. "Speaking of entertainment, want to come in awhile and watch TV?"

"Will your folks mind?"

Kasey laughed. "Get real, Ryan. My folks are crazy about you. My mom, anyway. And my dad doesn't think you're so bad either. Come on. We can fix some microwave popcorn and watch some gloppy flick on the late show."

"I'll pass on the late show. I don't want to sleep through church tomorrow morning. But I'll stay long enough for some popcorn."

"Right. I guess that old saying is true. The way to a man's heart is through his stomach."

"Like, it's true for me," agreed Ryan. "Give me some of my mom's homemade spaghetti, and I'm yours for life."

"Would you make the same deal for my family's spaghetti? In fact, maybe your mom's recipe is the same as my grandmother's."

"Could be. There must have been some great Italian chef a hundred years ago who started the whole thing and passed the recipe down to all our relatives. But for tonight, popcorn will do."

They went inside and headed for the kitchen. "My folks must already be in bed," said Kasey. "And I suppose Keith is still out with Laury."

"Those two are inseparable lately," said Ryan, removing a plastic pop bottle from the fridge and pouring two glasses of Pepsi.

"Does it bother you?" asked Kasey. "Seeing as how you and Laury went around together last year."

"No," said Ryan firmly. "We talked about this earlier. You know Laury and I were just friends."

"Not in her mind," argued Kasey. "Besides, I see the way Laury looks at you sometimes."

"Well, the way I see it, all she has eyes for now is your brother." Ryan returned the Pepsi bottle to the refrigerator. "Hey, Kasey, what's this?" he asked, removing a sheet of paper from under the magnet on the door.

"What? Oh, that note? Must be a message from my mom. What does it say?"

"It says, 'Kasey, Dusty Jernigan called. He's driving to Springfield to see you tomorrow. Says he has something important to tell you. Mom.'"

"Let me see that," said Kasey. She quickly read the note. "I don't understand. What could Dusty have to tell me?"

"Search me," said Ryan grimly. "Whatever it is, it sounds like trouble to me."

"Oh, Ryan, how can you say that? You don't even know what he's going to tell me." Kasey placed the popcorn bag in the microwave and turned it on, then turned back to Ryan. "It's probably nothing at all. My mom probably just made it sound like a big deal. You know how mothers are."

Ryan sat down at the table and turned his glass distractedly. "No, I got it figured, Kase."

She sat down across from him and sipped her drink. "You do? Tell me."

Ryan's dark brown eyes riveted on her with an intensity that unnerved her. "I bet he's coming here to ask you to marry him."

"Marry him?" Kasey choked on her drink, nearly spraying Ryan with Pepsi. "Come on, Ryan, give me a break!"

"I'm not kidding. What else could it be?"

Kasey wiped off her mouth and rolled her eyes in exasperation. "This is totally unreal, Ryan. I can't believe you'd think such a dumb thing. How many times do I have to tell you? Dusty and I are just friends."

"Right. Like Laury and me."

She eyed him doubtfully. "Are you saying you and Laury are more than friends?"

He sighed. "I'm saying she would like to be, just like Dusty would like to be. You give that guy an inch, and he'll take a mile."

"What makes you think I'd give him an inch?"

"You've given him more than an inch. You write him letters all the time. He comes here to see you. He lives in the same house with your grandparents. Face it, Kasey, he's already practically one of the family!"

"That's not fair." Kasey stood abruptly and went over to the microwave. The popcorn was done, the final kernels popping. She retrieved the poofed-out bag and carried it gingerly over to the table. She usually loved the hot, buttery taste of freshly popped corn, but right now her mind was on Ryan and his irrational jealousy. She sat down and pulled open the bulging bag of fluffy corn. "Have some," she said, pushing it toward Ryan.

"Thanks," he said, mimicking her sullen tone.

They ate in silence for a minute. Finally she said in a soft, incredulous voice, "Do you really believe Dusty is coming here to ask me to marry him?"

Ryan nodded. "Your mom's note says it's something important. What else could it be?"

"But marriage? I'm not even eighteen yet."

"No, but Dusty's twenty now, isn't he? And he's making good money working on your grandparents' farm."

Kasey traced a water ring on the table. "That's true. Dusty practically runs the farm these days. It's too much for Gramps to handle anymore."

"So you see? Dusty doesn't have years of schooling ahead. He's a farmer already established in his occupation. He's probably ready to settle down with a wife."

"But I'm not! I won't be ready to get married for years!"

Ryan gave her another of those penetrating glances. "And when you are ready, I hope it's me you marry, not that Dusty dude."

"For sure," Kasey said quickly. It occurred to her that Ryan was offering her his own tenuous, backhanded proposal, but she decided not to press the issue now.

Ryan helped himself to the popcorn. "Do you want me to be here tomorrow when Dusty arrives?"

"Why would you want to be here?"

"To run interference. Keep Dusty in his place. Remind him it's my girl he's messing with."

"He knows I'm your girl."

"He's sure got a funny way of showing it."

Kasey's patience was wearing thin. "Lighten up, Ryan, OK? Maybe it's nothing at all. Let's not spoil the rest of our evening over something so dumb as a note on the fridge."

"This isn't about a note on the fridge," he countered. "It's about Dusty. I can't help it, Kase. I see red when I think that he could just go and marry you, simple as that. He's old enough. He's got a job, money, stability. His future's already set. It'll be years before I'm in that position."

"Oh, so that's it."

"What's it?"

"What you're really sore about."

"I'm not sore about anything."

"Yes, you are. You resent the fact that Dusty can just go and get married if he wants to. But you can't. We can't. We've both got years of schooling ahead and no money. And no career in sight."

"OK, I admit it. But doesn't that bug you sometimes, Kasey?" Ryan grabbed a napkin and wiped the grease off his fingers. "Don't you want to get on with life and get things settled? You know. Who you're going to marry, what you're going to do. Don't you want to get into a real career and stop messing with boring classes and part-time jobs that pay minimum wage?"

"Of course. That's why I want Juilliard so badly. It's real. It's my ticket to a serious career in music. But it's not going to happen unless God works a miracle."

Ryan reached across the table for her hand. "God can do it, Kase. Maybe He will. But I just pray that God doesn't want you with someone like Dusty while I'm still trying to get my career off the ground."

"If God wanted me with Dusty, don't you think He'd let me know?"

"That's what I'm afraid of. That something will happen tomorrow that will change everything between us."

Kasey said softly, "I won't let it happen, Ryan. I love you. That's all there is to it."

He pressed her hand against his cheek. "I love you too, Kase. No matter what Dusty says or does tomorrow, you remember that I love you."

"I will," she whispered solemnly.

But that night, as Kasey drifted off to sleep, her dreams swept in with pastel visions of Dusty—his handsome face and muscular, roughhewn torso, his laughter, his deep, resonant voice, his warm, gentle touch. Kasey could almost smell the straw in his tousled hair and see the cool country breeze rippling his shirt. She could see the pasture and the meadow and the gardens and smell the fragrance of daffodils and new-mown hay.

She felt a strange, heady nostalgia, a yearning to be back with Dusty on her grandparents' farm, as she was last summer—the two of them walking hand in hand through the woods to the pond, or sitting on the split-rail fence by the barn, or swinging in the old oak swing on the front porch.

Then, even as Kasey savored the sweet, bucolic scenes with Dusty on the farm, her dream changed. Suddenly, she was moving in slow motion down a long, hazy corridor toward a room with a ceiling several stories high. Dusty was walking in step beside her, wearing a shiny black tuxedo. And, incredibly, she was wearing a flowing, satin wedding gown!

4

At breakfast the next morning, Kasey asked her mother about Dusty's phone call. "Exactly what did he say, Mom? How did he sound? What's so important that he has to drive here to tell me?"

"Goodness, all these questions!" Her mother passed her the scrambled eggs. "Well, let's see. He didn't tell me why he's coming, but it sounded serious, so I told him to come ahead. Did I goof, Kasey?"

"No, Mom, it's OK. I'm just really curious is all."

Her mother ran a hand through her short, coppery brown hair. Her sparkling hazel eyes looked troubled. "Whatever he's coming to tell you, I hope it's nothing upsetting. You've got enough on your mind coping with your last semester of high school."

Kasey nodded. "I guess I'll find out soon enough. He should be here about the time we get home from church."

Sure enough, Dusty was sitting on the porch steps waiting when they pulled into the driveway shortly after noon. He looked as strapping as a lumberjack, and his sturdy features were tanned a toasty brown. His walnut-brown hair was sun-washed and growing in unruly locks onto his forehead and over his collar. He looked more handsome than she remembered.

As Kasey got out of the car, she spotted Gramps's new pickup truck by the curb. Dusty must have borrowed it for the drive to Springfield. Obviously, Grams and Gramps had approved of his trip. As soon as Kasey started up the sidewalk, Dusty bounded toward her in his quick, easy strides. He swooped her up in his arms, lifting her feet off the ground. "How's my little Kasey?" he boomed.

"Super," she said breathlessly as he set her down and went to greet her parents.

Kasey's father, who always managed to look a little uncomfortable in his natty Sunday suit, shook Dusty's hand politely and kept his remarks sparse and to the point.

Dusty didn't seem to notice. He returned to Kasey's side, took her hand, and led her into the house as if she were the visitor.

"Have I ever missed you, gal," he said as he tossed his jean jacket on a chair.

"I've missed you too, Dusty," she said, feeling suddenly shy. What was a girl supposed to say to a man who was about to propose?

"Can I get you two anything to drink?" offered her mother from the kitchen. "I'll be working on dinner, but we have Coke, juice, coffee, iced tea—"

"Iced tea's fine with me," said Dusty. "With lots of ice." He ambled over to the couch and sat down, stretching out his long legs. Patting the spot beside him, he said, "Come over here, girl, and let me look at you."

Kasey sat down beside him. She was wearing her best dress, the blue one that brought out the color in her blue-gray eyes. And she had on her blue-tinted contact lenses that gave her eyes an extra sparkle. Her permed, wheat-colored hair was curled just right around her face, so she knew she looked her best. Why, then, did she feel so self-conscious, so tongue-tied? Why was her heart pounding so hard in her chest? Did these topsy-turvy sensations mean she actually loved Dusty more than Ryan? The thought sent a new wave of butterflies attacking her stomach.

"You look more beautiful every time I see you, Kasey," said Dusty, his eyes as warm as the summer sun. "Last summer when you first came to Middleton to stay with your grandparents, you were like an awkward, newborn colt, trying your legs, struggling to get your bearings. But now—look at you! All grown up. A real woman."

Kasey swallowed hard. She wasn't sure she was quite ready to be called a "real woman." She felt more comfortable with her mom's harmless tag "young lady."

"I'm the same as ever," she managed with a slight croak. "Plain, ordinary Kasey Carlone."

"Naw! There's nothin' plain or ordinary about you, girl. You're special. There's nobody else like you—I can vouch for that."

Kasey lowered her gaze. "There are lots of girls who are prettier—"

"Prettier maybe, but not one of a kind—a true-blue original." He chuckled. "You're even all decked out in blue. How about that?"

Kasey squirmed a little, feeling the perspiration bead on her forehead. What was she going to tell Dusty? How was she going to keep from hurting him? Or what if he knew something she didn't? What if God did want her to be with him? What if Dusty Jernigan was the man she was supposed to marry?

"No-o-o," she said, drawing the word out under her breath.

"No, what?" asked Dusty.

She looked at him, feeling momentary panic. "Nothing. I was just talking to myself."

"Well, shucks, girl, I do that all the time. Only usually I'm walking around on the farm, and only the cows are listening."

Kasey's mom brought their iced tea and a plate of crackers and cheese. "This should tide you two over until dinner," she said, stealing back to the kitchen as quickly as she appeared. Kasey almost wished her mother would stay so that she could postpone this serious discussion with Dusty. But then again, what was the sense in prolonging the inevitable? She decided to take the initiative.

"So what was it you wanted to tell me, Dusty?"

He looked at her. "Well, how about you? Coming right out with it. Getting right to the heart of the matter. You're becoming a lady with gumption, Kasey. I like to see good horse sense in a woman."

"It's not horse sense. It's called curiosity. I'm dying to know. What did you come here to tell me?"

"I'll get to it," he said, reaching for her hand. He interlocked their fingers and swung her hand up on his knee, tapping out a beat to music only he could hear.

"First, I wanted to bring you a greeting from Middleton. From your best friend."

"You mean Diana Morley?" She thought a moment. "Oh, that's right. You two have been going to the same church since last September. I guess you would be friends of a sort by now."

Dusty nodded. "Diana said to tell you she's planning to see you one of these days soon. She'll give you a call. In fact, she wished she could have come with me—"

"Oh, she should have," said Kasey. "We could have had a fabulous time together. We all—" Kasey let her words drift off as she recalled the serious nature of Dusty's visit. Diana Morley was the spoiled, vain, frivolous, impatient type. She would never have stood around waiting while Dusty and Kasey had a serious conversation. No, under the circumstances, it was better that Diana stayed home.

"How is Diana?" Kasey asked, reluctantly recalling her friend's cocaine problem and the trouble she'd got Dusty into last summer.

"She's doing real good," said Dusty. "She's been clean since last fall. She's in therapy and back in church. She's really trying to straighten her life out—square things with her family, with the community, and with God."

"I'm glad. I really am." Kasey looked carefully at Dusty. "And you don't hold a grudge against her after all she did to you, making it look like you were a thief when she was the one all along?"

Dusty chuckled. "Naw, we're a long way past that. All's forgiven and forgotten."

Kasey gave him a lingering glance. "You're really something, you know that? Most guys would have hated her forever."

"Not me. I gave up that hating business when I got to know the Lord. I figured if Jesus could love me even after my sins sent Him to the cross, then I don't have no business hating anybody."

Kasey smiled. "Like I said, Dusty, there's nobody quite like you."

"Ditto," he said. "Looks like we got us a mutual admiration society." He was still tapping their locked hands on his knee. "So now let me spit out what I wanna say, while I got the courage to say it."

Kasey's heart leaped. "Are you sure you want to, Dusty? I mean, maybe you should think about it a while—uh—give it more time."

"I don't need more time. I know my heart, and I know the time is right. And you've been one of the most important people in my life this past year, so it's time you know how I feel."

"I think I know," she said softly, averting her gaze.

"Really? You know?"

Kasey's heart was pounding harder now. Surely Dusty could hear it. What was a girl supposed to say at a time like this? *Lord, help me to know what to say,* she prayed silently.

Dusty was speaking. "So I guess you could see it in my face, right, Kasey?"

"What? See what?"

"Love. I figure it's written all over my mug. You figured it out. I'm in love."

"In love?" Somehow, Kasey couldn't get past stuttering silly monosyllables.

"Yeah, Kasey. I'm in love and wanna get married." Dusty said it with all the aplomb, naivete, and good-natured confidence of a leading man in a '40s flick. Like those dusty heroes of the black and white screen, Cary Grant and Clark Gable. As if there were no question about this love thing being reciprocal. "So what do you have to say, Kasey?" he urged. "Are you surprised?"

"Um, surprised? Yes, I am. For sure." More idiotic monosyllables!

Dusty released her hand at last and stretched his arms back over his head. "I never did think of myself as the marrying kind, but now that I'm not all bound up with hatred for my dad and the raw deal I got in life—well, now I got room inside for love. And, you know, it's a whole lot more pleasant than the bad feelings."

Kasey's palms were perspiring now. She wiped them on the sofa cushion. "Listen, Dusty, we've really got to talk about this."

"I know. That's why I'm here. To talk about the wedding."

"The wedding?" exclaimed Kasey, her voice rising shrilly. Her nerve ends were suddenly all on call. Waves of hot and cold rippled through her. Was this what they called a panic attack? "Dusty, how can you talk about the wedding when we haven't even sorted all this out yet? You know I'm going with Ryan Dimarco."

Dusty nodded. "That's fine. He can come too."

"Come where?"

"To the wedding."

"Dusty, don't you understand? There can't be any wedding!"

He looked at her, perplexed. "Sure there can. It's all set."

"Then you'll have to cancel it. You can't just plan a wedding without making sure you have a bride."

"I do have one. Diana said yes."

Kasey stared open-mouthed at Dusty. Suddenly everything clicked into place with horrifying clarity. "Diana? Diana Morley? You're marrying my best friend?"

He chuckled. "I guess I didn't make that clear, huh? Yeah, Diana and me are tying the knot. So tell me, what do you think?"

Kasey sank back into the sofa and closed her eyes. She had to bring her heartbeat down to legal speed before she could manage a reply. Somewhere in her head she could hear laughter. Ryan's laughter. The whole world laughing. *Hey, Kasey, you sure made a fool of yourself this time, thinking this dude wanted to marry you. Get real! You're still a kid. He wants a real woman!*

"So this is what you came to tell me," said Kasey weakly, "that you and Diana Morley are getting married?"

"Yes," said Dusty, his eyes as warm on her as ever. "You're my best friend, kiddo. You got my life on track. I owe you everything. I wanted you to be the first to know."

Kasey sat forward and studied a broken nail on her index finger. It had been her longest nail. When had she broken it? *Story of my life,* she mused.

"Are you listening, Kasey?"

"What?"

"I said, Diana and I want you in our wedding. She wants you to be her—what do you call it?—maid of honor."

"She does?"

"Yeah, she does. That's why she wanted to come too, so she could ask you in person. But we figured it was better this way. We didn't want to hit you with too much at once."

"No, that's OK," Kasey mumbled. But that's exactly how she felt. She'd been hit with too much—a speeding two-ton truck, a runaway locomotive, an exploding meteor. She felt shell-shocked, numb, disoriented. "So you and Diana are in love," she said, going back to square one. She had to make sense of that fact before she could go on to anything else.

"Yeah. Pretty crazy, huh?" mused Dusty. "Considering we were at each other's throats last summer."

"Right. You thought she was a total airhead, and she thought you were . . ." Kasey was about to say "the scum of the earth," but she let her words trail off. No sense in hurting Dusty's feelings—the way Kasey's were hurting right now.

"But, you see," Dusty rushed on excitedly, "Diana and I discovered we were both struggling with all these bad feelings about our families and our upbringing. We both had a lot to work through, and we figured it helped talking it out together. One thing led to another, and before we knew it all our negative feelings turned upside-down into a whole lot of positive feelings. Now all that's left to do is tie the knot and make it official."

"Then are you saying—you've already set a wedding date?"

"Sure have. This summer. The end of June. Soon as Diana gets her high school diploma."

"But I thought she was going on to college. She always wanted to go to college."

"Maybe someday. Between babies. Or when the kids are grown."

Kasey shook her head. "Are you sure we're talking about the same Diana Morley—party girl, poor little rich girl, Diana Morley?"

Dusty nodded. "Same girl. Only now she's into stability and security in her life. Me too. We wanna start putting down some roots, make our own home, start our own family. Have something good and solid that belongs to us."

"It sounds—wonderful," said Kasey. She felt unexpected tears well up in her eyes. Oh, no! She was going to cry. So far Dusty hadn't guessed her incredible blunder—that she had foolishly assumed he was in love with her. But if she burst into tears, he would know the truth and feel embarrassment and pity for her. She couldn't stand that. She jumped up from the sofa, dabbing at her eyes.

Dusty sprang up after her, as if on cue. "What's wrong, Kasey? Are you OK?"

She turned away quickly. "Never mind. You'd never understand."

5

Late that afternoon, after Dusty left, Kasey went to her room, locked her door, threw herself on her bed, and sobbed. She wasn't even sure why she was crying. It wasn't that she was in love with Dusty and wanted to marry him herself. Surely that wasn't the case. But maybe, in spite of herself, she had hoped that he loved her. Even counted on that love in some obscure way. After so many years of having no boy's attention, Kasey had found it flattering to know two boys cared for her—Ryan and Dusty. Dusty and Ryan. Two boys devoted to her, two boys who considered her special. Yes, she had thrived on their affection.

Now the truth was evident: she was no longer special to Dusty. She was just a friend. Perhaps he even saw her now as a little sister, someone to confide in, but not someone he wanted to kiss or hold. Why did it hurt so much to know that he didn't feel that way about her anymore? Where was this pain coming from? And why had she expected Dusty to remain devoted to her when she had made clear that Ryan was her first choice?

Come on, Kasey, get a life! You can dish it out, but you can't take it. The words assailed her with taunting persistence, but she angrily pushed them away. She wasn't in the mood to be sensible or rational. This had nothing to do with reason; it had everything to do with feelings, and right now she couldn't begin to make sense of her feelings.

And to make matters worse, it was her best friend Dusty was marrying. Somehow, a stranger would have been easier. Diana Morley had been Kasey's closest friend since grade school, but the two were nothing alike. While Kasey was shy and self-effacing, Diana was a go-getter who loved to toot her own horn. Kasey was the serious one; Diana the party girl. Diana was a little like Laury Lassen; she had the boldness and confidence to go after whatever she wanted, while Kasey usually hung back, struggling with inner doubts and misgivings.

Suddenly the phone rang, cutting into Kasey's thoughts. She sat up and hastily dried her tears. If it was for her, she didn't want anyone to know she was crying. A moment later there was a knock on her door, and her mother called, "It's for you, Kasey. Ryan."

Reluctantly Kasey picked up the receiver and said hello.

"Hi, Kase. How's it going?"

"OK. Why?"

"Dusty still there?"

"No. He left about an hour ago."

"Really?" Ryan sounded elated. "Man, I figured he'd hang around a while. Maybe even stay overnight."

"No. He had to get back to the farm. He borrowed Gramps's truck. Gramps will need it tomorrow."

"So tell me. What was the big deal?"

"What do you mean?"

"Dusty's important news. What was he dying to tell you?"

Kasey didn't answer.

"Hear me, Kase? What did he say? Did he propose, or what?"

"Propose? Really, Ryan!"

"OK, so he's not talking wedding bells then?"

"I didn't say that."

"Then he did talk about marriage!"

Kasey sighed. "Yes, he talked about it."

"I knew it! That guy has the hots for you. That friendship business was just a big sham, right?"

Kasey choked back a sob.

"Kasey? What's the matter? You sound like—hey, you're not crying, are you?"

"No, I'm not crying," she sniffled.

"Yes, you are. I can hear it in your voice. What happened? What'd that guy pull anyway?"

"Nothing. Just forget it, Ryan."

"Did he do something to hurt you? If he did—"

"No, Ryan, it's nothing like that. Listen, I've gotta go—"

"Wait, Kasey. Tell me. I bet he came on to you, didn't he? And when you told him where to get off, he got mean. Is that it?"

Kasey grabbed a tissue from her bureau and blew her nose. "No, Ryan. You're totally wrong about Dusty. We were both wrong."

Ryan paused a moment. "You're saying he doesn't want to settle down and get married?"

"Yes, he does. But not with me." Kasey sniffed loudly, then announced with an edge of misery, "Ryan, he's marrying Diana Morley, my best friend back in Middleton."

There was a long silence on the other end of the line, then sudden laughter. "Can you believe that!" exclaimed

Ryan. "Well, that's terrific. Way to go!" He paused. "Hey, you're not upset about this, are you, Kase? Kasey? You still there?"

"Yes, I'm still here."

"You are upset, aren't you? That's why you're crying. I thought you and this Dusty dude were only friends."

"We are."

"Then why are you so bent out of shape about him marrying your girlfriend back home?"

Kasey sniffed again. "I don't know, Ryan. Don't ask me to explain. I don't want to talk about it."

Ryan sounded sullen now. "You do love the guy, don't you?"

In a small, somber voice, she said, "Not like you mean, but, yeah, I guess in a way I love him."

Another lengthy pause, then: "Well, when you get your head on straight, give me a call." It wasn't Ryan's normal voice. His words were strangled, forced, too abrupt. "I gotta go get ready for church."

"Are you picking me up?"

"I don't know. Why don't you just ride with your folks?"

"I guess I could. But I thought you wanted to talk."

"No, I'm not in the mood for talking anymore."

"Ryan, are you mad at me?"

"Mad? Why should I be mad?"

"You are mad. I can tell."

"Naw. Just because my best girl gets all broken up over this dude marrying someone else? Just because she admits she loves the guy? Why should that make me mad?"

"Give me a break! It's not the same way I love you."

"Love is love. And right now you've got me wondering if you know the meaning of the word."

"I know it better than you do, Ryan Dimarco. If you loved me, you'd try to be understanding."

"And if you loved me, you wouldn't be crying over some other guy!"

"If—if that's the way you feel, Ryan—good-bye!" Without thinking, Kasey slammed down the receiver, then quickly picked it up again and listened. The dial tone! So Ryan had already hung up. He hadn't even waited to see if she was still on the line.

Kasey pushed the phone away and stretched out on her bed. Anger and anguish rumbled in her chest like a pot boiling over. She didn't know whether to cry, or scream, or throw something. She pounded her fist against her pillow, then pressed her fist against her mouth to keep back a shriek of rage. Then she sat up, hugged her pillow against her chest and rocked back and forth, sobbing. "Ryan—Dusty! Now I've lost you both!"

6

On Monday morning, Kasey dreaded facing her family at the breakfast table. She knew her misery was written all over her face. Her brother, Keith, a college freshman who still hadn't outgrown his Dennis the Menace image, was the first to comment.

"Hey, what's up, Goggles? What's got your chin draggin' the ground?"

"None of your business, Mooseface." She reached for the scrambled eggs, avoiding all eye contact.

"Don't have a cow," grumbled Keith. "I was just trying to show a little brotherly concern."

"And I'm the Queen of England in tennis shoes," snapped Kasey.

"Hey, you two, give it a rest," said Dad. Being out of work for more than four months had given an edge to her father's usually affable disposition. "Let's start this morning on a positive note, OK?"

Kasey and Keith both nodded, then looked daggers at each other when no one was watching.

"So, Goggles," said Keith with a sly smile, "did both your lover boys dump on you in the same day?"

Kasey looked urgently at her mother. "Mom, will you please tell Keith to lay off?"

"Keith," said Mom, "you heard your sister."

"I'm just showing a little friendly interest in her love life, Mom."

"Don't do me any favors, brother dearest," said Kasey thickly. "Do I go around asking you about your Madonna clone, Laury Lassen?"

"Kasey," said Mom. "Let's be kind."

"Scratch that last remark." Kasey pushed back her chair. "May I be excused, Mom? I'm really not hungry."

"All right, Kasey, but I'd like us to have a little talk tonight when you get home from school."

Kasey nodded, but she wasn't in the mood for a lecture from Mom. She was stressed out enough thinking about confronting Ryan today. Would he come by and pick her up for school the way he usually did? Would he even speak to her? Was their relationship finished? She grabbed up her books and wondered how she could have messed up everything with her two favorite guys in a single day without even trying.

"Listen, Mom," she said, hovering uncertainly in the doorway, "I may need a ride to school."

"Well, all right. I'm cleaning a house this morning, but I could drop you off on the way. But what about Ryan?"

Kasey bit her lower lip. "I don't think Ryan's coming by today."

"Wanna bet?" said Keith. "Listen, I hear his old clunker in the driveway right now."

Kasey ran to the window. Sure enough, it was Ryan's car. Her heart raced with excitement. "OK, great. Ryan's here. I guess I'd better run. So long, everyone!"

But when Kasey reached Ryan's car, her anticipation turned to dread. What could she possibly say to him after last night? What would he say to her? She opened the door and slipped inside just as she always did, but she managed only a sidelong glance his way.

"Hi," he said, putting the car in reverse.

"Hi. I wasn't sure you'd come by."

"I always do, don't I?"

"Yes, but I thought—I was afraid everything had changed."

He looked at her. "Do you want everything to change?"

She gazed down at the books in her lap. "No. I don't."

"Me neither." Ryan backed out into the street, shifted gears, and pushed his foot hard on the gas pedal. The car lurched forward and gained momentum quickly. "I'm willing to forget last night if you are, Kase."

Her voice wavered. "I want to forget, but I'm not sure I can. I really lost it. I'm sorry. I don't know what happened."

"I'm sorry too. I guess I wasn't much help in the sympathy department."

She managed a wan little smile. "Don't apologize. You'll just make me feel more guilty. I've been an absolute bear since yesterday—getting mad at you, fighting with my brother, sulking around the house, driving my parents crazy. I don't know what's wrong with me."

"I guess that Dusty dude meant more to you than you figured."

"I don't think that's it. Sure, I cared about him, and it was nice knowing he liked me—"

"Yeah? So? What else?"

With her fingernail she traced Ryan's name on her notebook cover. "And I admit I was shocked by his engagement to my best friend. But I think it's more than that. Something besides Dusty."

"Yeah? Maybe it's hormones or something."

"No way. I think it's more like—what do they call it?—'senioritis.' Everything's changing so fast. We have only a few months left of high school. Think about it. Our lives will never be the same."

He shrugged, keeping his gaze on the road ahead. "Not much we can do about it. We can't make time stand still."

"Sometimes I wish we could. And other times I wish we could speed it up and skip the hard years and start our real lives."

"Our real lives? What do you think this is—chopped liver?"

She laughed. "You know what I mean."

"Yeah. I know. And it's great to hear you laugh again." As he pulled into the school parking lot, he glanced over at her. "Shall we get together after school and pick up this laughter thing where we left off? We could stop for a pizza or something and talk about senior panic and laugh our heads off, if you want."

"Sounds super, as long as we stop laughing long enough to devour lots of pizza."

"Absolutely. Nothing like pizza with laughter mixed in. It'll cure senior panic every time."

As Ryan promised, after school that afternoon he drove Kasey to the Pizza Hut. They settled into a back corner booth and ordered Pepsis and a large pizza with the works. "Did you tell your mom you'd be late?" he asked as they sipped their soft drinks.

Kasey nodded. "I called her at lunchtime. I think she was relieved I was in a better mood. She said she wouldn't plan on me for dinner."

"Good. Then we have lots of time to talk."

Kasey looked curiously at Ryan. "There's something different in your voice. And in your eyes too. What's up?"

He chose his words carefully. "I've been thinking a lot about you and me and about what happened last night."

"You mean, about Dusty getting engaged?"

"Yeah. And your reaction to it. Did you stop to think, Kasey? Maybe, deep inside, you were wishing you were the one getting engaged."

"Me? To Dusty?"

"No, not to Dusty. To me."

Kasey sat back and took a deep breath. If she had ever felt speechless, now was the time.

Ryan was silent, too, while the waitress served their pizza. Then, while they each helped themselves to a steamy slice, he rushed on. "It makes sense, Kasey. We love each other. We've been going together over a year. And, like you said, after graduation everything's going to change. If we don't make a commitment now, maybe we'll drift apart. Break up for real. And after last night, I don't ever want to take a chance of losing you."

"Same here," said Kasey. "I felt so miserable last night, I nearly died. But marriage—"

"Not marriage. Not yet anyway. I'm talking about getting engaged, making things official. Lots of girls get engaged during their senior year."

Kasey looked quizzically at Ryan. "Tell me. Is this an official proposal—right here at Pizza Hut over a pizza with the works?"

He grinned. "No, Kase. This is all off the record. I'm just exploring our options. I'll plan moonlight and roses for the real thing."

"Good, because I was starting to get so many butterflies in my stomach, I was afraid this yummy pizza would go to waste."

They ate for a few minutes without speaking. Then Ryan said, "I've got it figured out."

"What?"

"Our future."

"You do?"

"Right. How does this sound? We get engaged at graduation, then we both work all summer and save our money. In the fall, we both start junior college and work part-time."

"OK, then what?"

"Then we get married next Christmas or next spring. We'll be old enough, Kase. You'll be eighteen, I'll be nineteen. We can rent a little apartment by the college. I'll work full-time and go to school part-time. You can still go to school full-time and get your degree."

"But what will you do? How will we have enough money?"

"No problem. I'll be a cashier at Kroger's. The pay's not bad, and I can still carry six units or more each semester at J.C."

"But what about your plans to be a doctor, or a teacher, or a missionary? And what about my dream of being a concert pianist?"

"Easy," said Ryan, undaunted. "After we finish junior college, we transfer to a university where we can get our degrees. Don't you see? We'll make our dreams come true, but we'll do it together."

Even in the dimly lit restaurant, Kasey could see the ardor and excitement in Ryan's eyes. "You really believe it could work?"

He took her hand and pressed it against his lips. "I'm sure of it, Kasey. If we want it enough, we can make it happen."

"I do want us to be together, but it's just so much to think about. My head's spinning."

"Well, we don't have to make any decisions now, Kase. But I want us to pray about it, because our whole future together is at stake."

Kasey shivered a little. She didn't want to think about their future's being at stake. If there was one thing she knew after last night, it was that she couldn't bear to risk losing Ryan.

"I'll pray about it, Ryan," she said fervently. "Boy, will I ever pray!"

7

When Kasey arrived home that evening, her mother was already cleaning up the dinner dishes. "Did you have a good time with Ryan?" she asked, wiping her hands on a dish towel.

Kasey nodded dreamily. Her mind was whirling with so many possibilities, it was hard even to concentrate on her mother's words.

"Let's sit down a minute, Kasey." Her mother motioned toward the kitchen table. "I'd like us to have a little talk."

Kasey sat down. "About Dusty?"

"Not exactly. About you."

Kasey sighed. "I'm sorry I acted so awful this morning, Mom. I don't know what got into me."

"I understand, honey. It was a surprise to learn that Dusty was engaged. I think you liked him a little more than you thought."

"I'm not sure, Mom. Sometimes, the older I get, the harder it is to know how I feel. One minute I feel one thing, the next minute I feel something entirely different. Is that normal?"

Her mother chuckled. "Yes, I'm afraid it is. It's part of growing up. The best thing you can do is pray the Lord guides you the way He wants you to go and gives you His desires for your life."

"I do, Mom. I pray every day. But sometimes I still feel confused."

"Me too. But that's where faith comes in. Don't worry, honey. God won't steer you wrong."

Kasey chewed thoughtfully on her lower lip. "But what about Dad? Wasn't he sure God wanted us to move to Springfield?"

"Yes. We were both sure God wanted us to leave Middleton two years ago and come here."

"But look what's happened. Dad lost his job and can't find a new one. You have to go out and clean houses so we can make ends meet. And there's not enough money now for me to go to Juilliard. Maybe we made a mistake coming here after all."

Kasey's mother moved her hand over the tabletop, pushing several stray bread crumbs into a little pile. "No, Kasey, I believe God wanted us here. But that doesn't mean His will is going to be easy. It just means we keep on trusting Him through the hard times."

"I think Dad's having a hard time trusting," said Kasey. "Sometimes he seems so angry and upset lately."

"I know, but he's trying his best. He hasn't mentioned it to the family yet, but he'd like to open his own Mini-Mart."

"You mean one of those little markets with groceries and stuff?"

"Yes, he would manage it himself like he ran the general store back in Middleton. You know how he loves being his own boss."

"It sounds great, Mom. Why doesn't he do it?"

"Because it would take too much money. So you see, he has his dream like you do, but he can't afford it either. That's why he's frustrated. He just doesn't know what the future holds for him."

"Join the club," said Kasey under her breath.

"I know. It's hard for all of us, but we've got to be as supportive of your dad as we can right now."

"I'm doing all I can, Mom. I gave up my hopes of going to Juilliard, didn't I?"

Her mother tapped her fingers on the table. "Speaking of Juilliard, this letter came for you today." She reached over to the counter for an envelope and handed it to Kasey.

"It's—it's from Juilliard." Awestruck, Kasey tore open the envelope, her fingers suddenly weak and fumbling. Eagerly she scanned the letter. "Mom, listen to this. It's about my application status. It says I'm accepted for the fall semester, contingent on my final high school transcripts."

"Oh, Kasey, really? You did it! I'm so proud of you!" Her mother's radiant smile faded suddenly. She sat back and sighed. "So it's official. You really could have gone to Juilliard."

Kasey felt her sinuses fill and a lump grow in her throat. She didn't want to cry in front of Mom. She stood up, clutching the envelope against her chest. "I've got to be alone a while, Mom, OK?"

"Sure, Kasey." Her mother reached out and took her hand. "Honey, listen. I'm sorry we can't afford to send you. I'm so sorry we can't make your dream come true."

"It's OK, Mom. Really, it's OK." Kasey turned and ran upstairs to her room and shut the door. She curled up on her bed and hugged her pillow against her chest. *No,*

Mom, it's not OK! It'll never be OK! I wanted Juilliard so bad I could taste it!

Kasey heaved a sigh of despair. Here she was sobbing again, for an entirely different reason than last night! Why did so many things have to happen at once to turn her life upside-down? Why couldn't she just have been rejected by Juilliard? Then she wouldn't feel so bad about not being able to afford to go!

She sat up and reached for the Juilliard catalog on her bureau. With an ache of yearning she thumbed through it as she had so many times before, dreaming of the day when she might actually be a student there. How many times had she imagined herself at the Juilliard campus in Lincoln Center, visiting the Metropolitan Opera House or the New York State Theater, hearing the New York Philharmonic Orchestra or seeing the New York City Ballet? She probably would have lived in the Juilliard residence hall with other students who loved classical music as much as she did. Even Juilliard's address sounded magical and inviting: On Broadway, just two blocks west of Central Park, in the heart of New York City.

Kasey gazed longingly at the catalog photographs of students singing and dancing and performing. They were the lucky ones—the ones who had made it, who had the talent and the money to turn their dreams into reality. She flipped through to the financial aid section. Surely there were grants, scholarships, or loans that could enable her to attend. But no, even they couldn't cover the $20,000 Kasey would need for room, board, and tuition each year.

How could she even think of spending so much money when her father couldn't stretch his unemployment checks to cover house payments and utilities? How could she expect a miracle for herself when her father's career goals still remained distant and unreachable?

Kasey put away the catalog and dried her eyes. She went over to her desk, sat down, and took out her pen and stationery. There was only one thing she could do: write Juilliard and tell them she was withdrawing her application.

8

When Kasey said good night to her parents that evening, she gave her mother the letter she'd written to Juilliard. "I've withdrawn my application," she told them, wincing at the expression of regret in her parents' eyes.

"You know how sorry we are," said her father, looking up from his newspaper. His eyes glistened, and his voice sounded gravelly. "If there were any other way, Kasey—"

"It's OK, Dad," she said, hugging him.

"Do you want me to mail this for you?" asked her mother.

Kasey nodded. "Would you, Mom? I just can't do it myself."

Her father was about to say something else, but the phone rang, and he went to answer it. After a moment, he said, "Kasey, it's for you."

She looked quizzically at him. "Who would be calling this late at night? Is it Ryan?"

"No. It's a woman. I don't recognize the voice."

Kasey took the receiver and said, "Hello?"

A formal, strongly accented voice said, "Is this Miss Carlone? Miss Kassandra Carlone?"

"Yes—"

"Was your picture in the *Springfield Times* last September? A photograph of you with a woman from the Shady Oaks Retirement Home?"

"Yes, but—"

"A Jewish woman named Olive Solomon?"

"I'm sorry, I don't understand. Who's calling, please?"

The voice softened. "My name is Bessie Golden. I am calling from Pasadena, California." She hesitated a moment, then said, "Is it late there? Oh, my goodness, I did forget about the time difference."

"It's nearly eleven," said Kasey. What a time for a crank call!

"I am so sorry, Miss Carlone. It is not quite nine here. I did not mean to disturb you. Perhaps I should not have called, but I had to know—"

"It's OK," said Kasey. "What about Olive Solomon? Do you know her?"

"Yes, I believe so. I am not sure. Someone sent me the article from the newspaper—a friend visiting the Midwest. She read the article and saw the resemblance, but then she misplaced the paper. When she found it again, she sent it to me. But it's been so long. I would have called you months ago."

"I'm sorry," said Kasey. "I'm really confused."

"Of course you are, dear. I'm rambling. I am nervous, you see. The article about Shady Oaks has done this to me. I am trying to remain calm. But when I saw the picture I knew—"

"Knew what?" asked Kasey.

The woman's voice grew tremulous. "I knew—I knew I had found my sister."

Kasey's thoughts snapped to attention. "Your sister? Olive Solomon? But it can't be. Her whole family is dead!" Kasey stopped and swallowed her words. She hadn't meant to blurt out the truth so rudely.

"Dead?" echoed the woman. "They are all dead?"

"Yes," said Kasey solemnly. "They—they died in the concentration camps during the war."

The woman's tone turned steely. "I know, child. I was in the death camp with Olive in Poland in 1944, but we were separated. I was sent to another camp in Germany. Eventually I escaped. I assumed all my family had died—until I saw the photograph of Olive Solomon."

"What makes you think she's your sister?" asked Kasey.

A pause, then: "Because when I look at her picture, it is like looking into a mirror."

Kasey felt a cold shiver travel along her spine. Obviously this was no crank call after all. "How can I help you, Miss Golden?"

"I called you because I do not want to contact my sister until I am sure it is she. My sister's name was Olive Golden. She was not married. She was a wonderful singer."

"Well," said Kasey, "Solomon is Olive's married name, and she was a famous opera singer after the war."

The woman's voice throbbed with hope. "She does indeed sound like my sister. If I could only be certain. Wait, there is something—"

"What?" asked Kasey.

"My sister wore the dreaded tattoo that we Jews were forced to wear in those days—a number on her left forearm a few inches above the wrist. Have you seen that mark?"

"Yes, of course, I have," said Kasey. "I even know the number."

"Listen to me, Miss Carlone. I will tell you my sister's number, and you will know if she is this Olive Solomon. Is the number—553668?"

"Yes!" said Kasey, feeling another chill, more awesome than the first. "That's the number. Olive Solomon is your sister!"

For a minute there was absolute silence on the other end of the line. Kasey wondered if the woman had hung up, but then she heard a deep sob. Finally the woman spoke again, her voice choked with emotion. "I will come to Springfield this weekend. I will make reservations to fly there. I want very much to see my sister, but first I would like to talk with you, Miss Carlone. I would like you to prepare my sister for my visit. I do not want to shock her or upset her in any way."

"I'm sure she'll be totally thrilled to see you," said Kasey, "but, sure, I'll be glad to break the ice for you and tell you whatever I can about Olive. She's a wonderful lady, almost like a grandmother to me."

"I sensed that about you, Miss Carlone. I am looking forward to meeting with you. I will call you when I arrive in town."

"OK, that sounds great," said Kasey. "Good-bye, Miss Golden."

She hung up the phone and turned to her parents. They were both watching expectantly, waiting for an explanation. She repeated what Bessie Golden had said.

"It looks like you'll have a chance to play an important role in reuniting these sisters," said her mother with a smile.

Kasey nodded. "Just think. They haven't seen each other in almost fifty years. Can you imagine?"

"They'll have a lot of time to make up for," said her father.

"But you know what, Dad?" said Kasey. "I just wish there was some way that finding her sister again would soften Olive's heart to the Lord."

"Who knows? Maybe God will use this to reach her," said Mom. "We'll all have to keep Olive and her sister in our prayers."

"Meanwhile, I'm going to hit the sack and concentrate on dreamland," said Dad, kissing Kasey good night.

"I'm tired too," she said, heading toward the stairs. But she had a feeling she was going to be too keyed up to sleep. So, instead of climbing into bed, Kasey put on a Dino tape, opened her curtains, and sat down by the window. As she gazed out at the starry sky, she whispered a prayer to God, pouring out her anguish over not going to Juilliard and her confusion about Ryan and Dusty. She prayed for her father's dream of opening his own Mini-Mart and for the woman in Pasadena who was Olive Solomon's long lost sister.

"Lord Jesus," she said softly, "there are so many things happening right now to people I love. And so many decisions to be made. Help me to know if Ryan is the one you want me to marry. He says he wants us to get engaged, but it's such a big step, and I'm really scared. But I love him and never want to lose him, and now that You've shut the door on Juilliard—are You trying to tell me that marriage is Your will for me instead of a career in music? Please, help me to know what to do—and be with Olive Solomon when she meets her sister again for the first time in so many years. Somehow, help Olive to know that You love her."

After talking over her problems with the Lord, Kasey felt as if a burden had been lifted from her shoulders. She felt relaxed for the first time that day. Perhaps her problems still had no permanent solution, but at least for tonight she could sleep soundly.

The following Saturday morning, Kasey received another phone call from Bessie Golden. She wasn't calling from Pasadena this time but from the Holiday Inn in Springfield. "I would like you to come have lunch with me here at the restaurant, Miss Carlone, if you are free. I would like to talk more with you about my sister."

"I'd like that," said Kasey. "If I can borrow my brother's car, I can be there in about an hour."

"Oh, I will send a taxi for you, if you wish."

"No, that's OK. I'll see you at the restaurant in an hour."

Kasey arrived at the restaurant just before noon, and as soon as she walked in the door, she spotted Bessie Golden standing ramrod straight beside a planter of tropical greenery. Bessie was a younger, trimmer version of Olive Solomon. She had black hair streaked with gray and pulled back neatly in a bun. Her eyes were snapping black like Olive's and her brows thick and bristly. Her face was lined with pain but glowed with the wisdom of the ages. Kasey had no doubt that this was indeed Olive Solomon's sister.

The woman met Kasey's gaze for a moment, then looked beyond her at other passersby.

Kasey walked directly over to her and smiled. "Hello, Miss Golden? I'm Kasey Carlone."

The woman smiled with obvious embarrassment. "I thought it was you, my dear, but I wasn't sure. The girl in the newspaper clipping wore glasses."

"Right. But I wear contacts now."

"Well, you are a very attractive young lady. Come. I have a table reserved." She motioned toward the hostess. "My party is here now. May we please be seated?"

They followed the hostess to a small, linen-draped table set with china and silver, with a vase of fresh flowers in the center.

"It looks beautiful," said Kasey, sitting down. The hostess handed them menus and told them a waitress would take their order in a minute. Privately, Kasey wondered if Bessie Golden planned to pay for their meal. One look at the prices told Kasey she herself could never afford it.

She was relieved when Miss Golden said, "Order anything you like, dear. It is my treat. To thank you for helping me find my sister."

"I'm so excited about this," said Kasey. "Your sister is a very special person. Like I told you on the phone, she's been like a grandmother to me."

"She was always special," said Bessie wistfully. "She had a voice like an angel. But then everyone in our family was talented. We lived in Poland and had a very good life. A beautiful home that had been in our family for many generations. My father was a professor in the university. My mother was a painter. I thought life would always be wonderful for us—until the soldiers came and took us from our home and put us on the train for Auschwitz."

"Is that where your family was taken?"

"Yes. Hasn't Olive told you about it? She was twenty-two, and I was eighteen. We were herded with hundreds of others into a freight train. We were so crowded together we could only stand. Some were nearly crushed. We could hardly breathe. But that was only the beginning—"

"You didn't remain with your family at Auschwitz?"

"Only for a while. Then many of us were transported to Ravensbruck, an extermination camp in Germany. The Nazis evacuated many people from the death camps in Belgium, France, Poland, Holland, and Austria. They took us to a worse death hole in the heart of Germany. I suppose they thought they could hide their evil deed by bringing us to one central place in their country."

"Olive never talks about it," said Kasey. "She's told me a little, but no details. It's too painful for her to mention."

"It was painful for me, too," said Bessie, "but I have forced myself to talk. If we do not talk, no one will know. No one will believe what happened. And one day, we who suffered such atrocities will all be gone, and then who will tell people? Who will warn them what can happen when people surrender to the evil within them?"

"I never thought of it like that," said Kasey.

Their waitress came then and took their order, so all talk of the death camps ceased. Bessie ordered poached salmon, and Kasey ordered veal scaloppine, which came with cream sauce, mushrooms, and fettuccine. It tasted scrumptious.

As they ate, Bessie said, "Tell me about my sister. How is her health? How are her spirits?"

"She's doing OK," said Kasey, wrapping the creamy pasta around her fork. "I think she's had some heart trouble, but I don't know much about it. When I met her she was very lonely and withdrawn, like a recluse. And very bitter about life. But since she began to sing again, she's come out of her shell. She likes people again."

"She still sings? Oh, I would love to hear her."

"She sings sometimes at the community center when Shady Oaks puts on one of their musicals or variety shows. In fact, she'll be singing next Friday night."

"Oh, I must hear her. But I must ask a favor of you, dear."

"Sure, if I can."

Bessie's face grew animated. The deep lines seemed to vanish. Her countenance glowed. "Will you tell her about me? Tell her gently so the shock will not be too great. Tell her on Friday night after she has performed. I will be in the audience. And after you have told her, I will come backstage to see her."

Kasey nodded. "I guess that would be OK. I just hope I can find the right words."

Bessie smiled. "You will, child. I know that about you already."

9

It was only seven, and already a crowd was gathering outside the Springfield Community Center. Many were senior citizens, of course, but there was a surprising number of families and young people.

"Looks like the Good Time Shady Oaks Players are getting more popular all the time," Ryan told Kasey as they threaded their way into the foyer.

Kasey laughed. "Let's face it—George Burns and his generation are in!"

Ryan edged carefully around a rotund lady with a menagerie of youngsters in tow. "We should have gone in the back way, Kase. We could have avoided—what'd that writer call it?—the madding throng."

"But then I couldn't have spotted Bessie Golden. I want to make sure she's here before I spring the news on Olive that her sister's alive."

"Do you see her?"

"Not yet."

"We can't wait. We've got stuff to do." Ryan clasped Kasey's hand as they wended their way backstage. "I don't know why that woman didn't just go over to Shady Oaks and see Olive the minute she got in town."

"I don't know either, Ryan. Except that she really wants to see Olive perform, and I think she was afraid Olive wouldn't if she knew her sister was in the audience."

Ryan shrugged. "Who can figure 'em? Only problem is, now you gotta be the go-between. What if Olive is so shocked she has a heart attack or something?"

"I know. That's what scares me too." Kasey raised her finger to her lips. "Shh. Olive's over there talking with Mrs. Smolin. I don't want them to know yet about Bessie. Now what do we need to do before showtime?"

Before Ryan had a chance to reply, Kasey was surrounded by her friends from Shady Oaks. Mr. Griley hobbled over with his accordion and rasped, "When do I go on? Before or after Mrs. Hyson's reading?"

"After," said Kasey.

Mr. Griley's wrinkled face clouded. "That's a shame. After Mrs. Hyson finishes her passage from Shakespeare, half the audience will be asleep."

Mrs. Hyson tapped her cane noisily on the hardwood floor. "I heard that, Mr. Griley. I tell you, old man, if you think you're another Lawrence Welk with your snazzy accordion, you got another think coming."

"Think, think, think! Ha! Where am I going to put another think from you, Mrs. Hyson!"

Miss Brummett stepped between them, waving a clipboard. "I have the performance schedule right here. Mrs. Pinkelman and Mr. Dowling will start with their Abbott and Costello routine. Then, Kasey, you will play a Beethoven sonata. Is that right?"

"Yes. No. 8 in C Minor, Opus 13. It's called 'Pathetique.'"

"And then Olive Solomon will sing one of her favorites—Puccini's *La Boheme-mi Chiamano Mimi*."

"Don't forget me," said Mrs. Tisdale. "I'll be playing my violin. 'Till the End of Time.'"

"Oh, my goodness, I hope not that long," said Mr. Suttles.

"That's my song title, my dear man."

"I'm not your dear man, Mrs. Tisdale. Or anyone else's."

"That suits me just fine, Mr. Suttles."

"But I will speak my mind," he continued, pointing a knobby finger at Kasey and the others. "We have entirely too many highbrow, long-hair selections tonight. This isn't the Metropolitan Opera."

"And it's not the Grand Ol' Opry," countered Miss Brummett. "Besides, Mr. Suttles, the Venerable Skewbald Band will be playing 'On the Atchison, Topeka and the Santa Fe.' And you'll be doing a soft-shoe to 'Don't Fence Me In.' That should balance things out quite nicely. A taste of the sublime and a touch of the ridiculous."

Kasey spoke up. "I think what Miss Brummett means is, we've got a good mixture of highbrow and lowbrow. Come on, folks! Let's go put on a show!"

The program went without a hitch, much to Kasey's relief. Somehow, since the old-timers' first talent show last year, Kasey and Ryan had been designated unofficial directors of the Shady Oaks Players. They were still learning on the job, just as the old folks were still honing their long-dormant talents. But it seemed to be a winning combination. Nearly every performance received a standing ovation. And what pleased Kasey most tonight was that she spotted Bessie Golden in the second row applauding louder than anyone else.

"That was a terrific job," Kasey told everyone afterward, as she made her way back to Olive Solomon's dressing room. She looked back at Ryan as he helped Mr. Griley put away his accordion, and mouthed the words *Pray for me!* Now if only she could find the words to tell Olive that her sister was still alive!

She knocked soundly on the door until she heard Olive say, "Come in." Then she entered, her heart pounding violently in her ears.

Olive was sitting at her dressing table wiping the rouge off her cheeks. "Look, Kasey, it is too much. Too red. I looked like a circus clown tonight."

"No, you looked beautiful, Mrs. Solomon. And you sounded wonderful."

Olive ran her hands over her throat. "Sometimes I think I still have the magic. Other times I am afraid it is gone."

Kasey sat down beside her. "Mrs. Solomon, I have something to tell you. But I'm not sure how to begin."

Olive looked closely at her. "Is it my performance? Did I—as you say—goof?"

"No, I meant what I said. You were wonderful. This is something else. Something I have to tell you."

"Well, what is it, child?"

"It's good news," said Kasey. "The best news in the whole world."

Olive chuckled. "All right. Tell me this good news."

Kasey drew in a deep breath. "It's about what happened to you during the war. In the concentration camps."

Olive stiffened and shook her head. "No, I do not talk about that."

"But we must," said Kasey. "You thought all your family died—"

"Yes. They all died. But why do you bring this up now, child?"

"Because—" Kasey moved closer to Olive and said in a small voice filled with wonder, "Because your sister Bessie did not die. She escaped. She is still alive."

Olive stared at Kasey with stark, stunned eyes. "What are you saying? Why do you taunt me with such words?"

"It's true," said Kasey. "Your sister is alive. She's here tonight at the community center. She wants to see you."

Olive's stooped frame shook. She clasped her arthritic hands together in a gesture of supplication. "Oh, if only God could make it so!"

"She's here," Kasey said again, putting her hand on Olive's shoulder. "Do you want me to bring her in?"

Olive looked around as if waking from a dream. "You say she's here? My sister? Bessie?"

Kasey went to the door and opened it. "Ryan, is Bessie nearby?"

Bessie Golden stepped forward, clutching a small handbag, standing tall in a silk flowered dress. "Yes, I am here. I want to see my sister."

At the sound of Bessie's voice, Olive Solomon stirred. "Bessie?" She stood, reached for her cane, and shuffled toward the door on her thick, stubby legs. "It can't be my sister. My sister is dead."

"No, Olive. It's me, Bessie. I'm alive. As alive as you are!"

Kasey stepped back and watched as the two women stared wordlessly at each other. Incredibly, they were mirror images. One was a little older, the other a little taller, but the faces were the same, mapped with profound loss and a brave history. As comprehension swept over Olive, she reached out and enveloped Bessie in her arms, rocking back and forth as if comforting a child, whispering words full of love in a language Kasey couldn't understand.

10

The two women wept in each other's arms for several minutes. Kasey felt self-conscious watching, but just as she was about to slip away, Olive Solomon reached out for her and said, "Wait, child. Do not go. You are the one who has brought my sister to me."

"Yes," said Bessie. "We want you to share these precious moments with us."

"OK, if you're sure." Kasey closed the dressing room door to keep out the backstage commotion and pulled up a straight-back chair. Olive and Bessie sat down side by side at the dressing table, still holding hands.

"Now," said Olive, her voice resonant with emotion, "tell me how you did this, Kasey. How did you find my sister?"

"Actually, she found me."

"Yes," said Bessie. "A friend came across the old newspaper clipping of you, Olive, in the *Springfield Times* last September. You were standing with Kasey on the porch at your retirement home. She sent it to me because the photograph looked so much like me. She wondered if we could be related. I saw the resemblance and immediately thought of you, Olive. Remember how people said we looked like twins?"

"Indeed, I do. But you were the younger, prettier one."

"And you were the talented one. You still have the voice of an angel." She dabbed at her moist eyes with a hanky. "At any rate, until I saw that clipping I thought you had died at Auschwitz."

"And I thought you died there too. After those first days, I never saw you again."

"I was taken to Ravensbruck."

"Oh, Bessie, no! The dreadful women's extermination camp! How did you survive?"

"I became a tutor for a German officer's children. They came to love me, so their father spared my life and helped me to escape just before the war ended."

Olive shook her head in amazement. "I was saved because of my voice. I am ashamed to say it, but I sang for the Nazis, Bessie. I sang for the murderers of our family. And I have lived with the guilt all of my life."

Bessie reached over and put her hand on Olive's cheek. "You should not feel guilty, dear sister. You were strong enough to find a way to survive. You should be proud."

"Did you feel no guilt?" asked Olive. "No anger that you survived when all the others did not?"

"Yes, I felt guilty—and angry. But I have learned not to dwell on those feelings. Now I concentrate on the goodness of God and not the evil of mankind."

Olive nodded. "Yes, for many years I was very bitter, but my little friend here helped me see that there is still much good about life. Didn't you, Kasey?"

Kasey smiled. "I just tried to show you God's love."

Bessie straightened her shoulders and lifted her chin high. "That is something I have come to know very well too, Olive."

"What, Bessie?"

"God's love. He has become very real to me in recent years."

Olive shrugged. "I no longer blame God for what evil people did to us, but I do not go to synagogue. I do not follow the religion of our people."

A wariness crept into Bessie's voice. "There is something I must tell you, dear sister. I hope you will understand."

"What? What could you possibly tell me now that I would not understand?"

Bessie squeezed Olive's hand tightly. "I have become what is called a 'completed Jew.' I have accepted Jesus Christ as my Messiah."

Kasey and Olive both stared at Bessie. Her pale lips trembled a little, but her dark eyes shone with peace.

Olive stiffened. "How could you turn to the Gentile's religion after all you suffered at their hands?"

Bessie's voice was tremulous but filled with conviction. "It was a Christian family that helped me escape the Nazis. The German officer whose children I cared for—he put me in touch with them. They all risked their own lives to save me."

"But to repay them by forsaking your own religion, your heritage, your birthright—!"

"No, dear Olive, I have not forsaken my birthright. My religion is complete now, because I have found the Messiah we have looked for all these years."

"I do not want to hear of it," said Olive abruptly. "We will not talk about such things."

Bessie nodded. "I only wanted you to understand why I am at peace now."

Olive reached for her cane and struggled to her feet. "Where are you staying, Bessie?"

"At the Holiday Inn here in Springfield."

"How long will you stay?"

Bessie stood up too. "That is up to you, sister."

Olive's voice softened. "We have so much to talk about. So much time to make up for."

"I am thinking of renting an apartment here in town," said Bessie. "I would like to stay a while so that we can be together."

Olive brightened. "I would like that very much. But do you have family or a job? Can you simply pack up and leave your home?" She paused and winced. "I know so little about you, sister. I do not even know where you have come from."

"California," said Bessie. "I am retired. I taught school for many years. I never married. So there is no one to consider but myself. And now you."

"Then we will be together, whatever it takes," said Olive with feeling. "We will never let anyone separate us again."

Later that evening, as Ryan drove Kasey home from the community center, she was jubilant. "Can you believe it, Ryan? Those two dear old ladies together again after all these years? And what's so terrific, Bessie is a Jewish Christian. It's totally perfect. She'll be able to help Olive see her need of Christ. I tell you, I am so up I feel like I'm freefalling through space."

He laughed, keeping his gaze on the road ahead. "You get any higher, babe, and I'll have to tie anchors on your feet."

"Don't you feel the excitement, Ryan? You saw how happy they were. We had a part in that. It was a miracle, and God let us share in it."

"Right. I'm happy for them. The whole thing's totally awesome." He shifted, slipping his arm around her shoulder and pulling her close. "But right now I want to concentrate on the good feelings I have for you."

She snuggled up against him and smiled. "Me too, Ryan."

They rode a while in silence. A Dino tape was playing, one of Kasey's favorites. The car engine hummed, lulling her mind to the edge of sleep. She loved moments like this, being close to Ryan, feeling safe and protected and loved. She wished times like this could last forever. Everything was so right, so exactly perfect.

Ryan pulled into her driveway and turned off the engine and lights. "Kase? You're not falling asleep, are you?"

"No," she whispered. "Just savoring the moment."

"That's what I want to do too." He turned her face up to his and kissed her lips, his mouth barely touching hers. His breath was minty and sweet and warm. "I love you, Kase. I wish I didn't have to leave you tonight."

"Same here," she murmured, feeling deliciously lightheaded. She loved the cocoon warmth of his torso as his arms enveloped her. They were so close she could nearly feel his heartbeat through his shirt.

Ryan kissed her again, harder, his mouth more demanding. After a minute, she pulled back, trying to catch her breath. "Ryan," she stammered. The automobile was suddenly too warm, too confining. She wriggled out of his grasp. "I'd better go in, Ryan."

He released her and sighed deeply. "I hate this. Always having to say good night just when I want you the most."

She moved away from him, straightening her clothes. "I know, Ryan. I feel the same way."

"I doubt it."

She looked at him. "Why does dating have to be so hard? Right when everything's going so good, it all changes. Suddenly we're both uptight and frustrated."

He ran his hand over the leather covering on his steering wheel. "If we were like most couples, we wouldn't fight it. We'd just do it without thinking about it. No big deal."

"But it is a big deal, Ryan. It's our special gift for the person we marry someday. And if we give it away now, we can never get it back."

Ryan rubbed her neck gently. "I know you're right. But sometimes I don't care about who I marry someday. I just want to love you now."

She shivered a little and closed her eyes. "I feel that way too, and I just have to keep telling myself I'm going to do the right thing, no matter how I feel. And the right thing now means going inside before I can't say no anymore."

She started to reach for the car door, but he caught her hand. "Listen, Kase, I haven't had the courage to mention it, but, uh, do you remember what I said to you a week or so ago?"

"What you said?"

"You know."

"About getting engaged?"

"Right. Have you—you know—thought about it?"

"How could I think about anything else?"

"And?"

"And what?"

He shrugged. "I don't know. Made any decisions? Had any great flashes of insight about our future?"

"Not really," she admitted. "Except, the more I know about life, the more I know I don't know."

"What's that supposed to mean?"

"See? I don't know."

"Well, here's what I know. We gotta go forward or backward. We can't remain static."

"Translate," she said softly.

"Meaning, we're either going to get more committed to our relationship—or less committed. If we don't move forward, we're losing ground. And who knows where we'll be then?"

Kasey looked at Ryan, searching his eyes. The moonlight and shadows cut strange patterns across his face, but it was still the most handsome face she had ever seen. "Ryan, all I can say for sure right now is that we're two months away from our high school graduation. Two months away from starting the rest of our lives. And I've never felt more confused about what I'm supposed to do. I pray about it and ask God to show me, and it's like He's not saying anything, like He's leaving it all up to me to figure out. I love you, Ryan, but it's not enough. I've got to know for sure in my heart that God wants us together."

Ryan sat back and crossed his arms on his chest. He made a little coughing sound low in his throat. "I'm not trying to pressure you, Kase. I want God's will as much as you do."

"Then maybe we should spend more time talking to Him together."

He grinned. "Why couldn't I have been the one to suggest that?"

"Doesn't matter who suggests it, as long as we do it."

"For sure." He reached over and took her hand. "When nothing else works, try praying, right?"

She smiled. "Better yet, try praying first."

11

When Kasey and Ryan visited Shady Oaks the following weekend, they discovered that Olive Solomon wasn't there. "Did she go out with her sister for the day?" Kasey asked Clarisa Huckabey, the house manager.

"Not only did she go out with her, she moved in with her!" said Clarisa with a twinkling smile. Clarisa always looked like she had a secret she was dying to tell. And now was no exception. "Can you imagine? After all those two women have been through, it's a miracle they found each other. Think of the stories they have to tell!"

"Wait. You say Olive moved in with Bessie?" persisted Kasey. "How?"

"Oh, well, her sister rented an apartment a few miles from here, and she marched in the other day and moved Olive and her things out. Just like that. Said she and Olive were going to make up for lost time, and the best way to do that was to move in together. I've got the address if you'd like to pay them a visit."

Kasey looked at Ryan. "Is it OK? After we've spent a while with the old folks here?"

He nodded. "We'd better telephone first. Make sure they want company."

When Kasey telephoned, Bessie didn't hesitate a moment. "Yes, come right over. I'll put on some tea. Or, I suppose you young people would rather have a soft drink."

"Don't fuss," said Kasey. "We just want to see you both."

Bessie's apartment was in a modern, tree-lined complex in one of Springfield's most expensive neighborhoods. There were lots of flowers and green grass everywhere, and each unit had its own little balcony. "Oh, I bet Olive loves it here," said Kasey as she and Ryan approached the front door.

Bessie let them in. She was wearing a frilly apron over her housedress, and she was beaming. "Welcome, children. You are our first guests."

"Boy, does it smell great in here," said Ryan, his gaze already riveted on the kitchen.

"Ah, when I knew you were coming, I baked chocolate chip cookies. Not my own homemade ones, I'm afraid. I didn't have time for those, but the cookies in those long plastic tubes that look like sausages. I hope they are acceptable."

"Don't worry. Ryan will eat anything." Kasey laughed, and they followed Bessie into the living room where Olive was sitting on the sofa with a crocheted afghan over her lap. Her complexion looked startlingly pale, but she was smiling.

"Kasey, come sit by me. Tell me how things are at Shady Oaks."

Kasey relayed the greetings of Olive's many friends from the retirement home, plus what scant news she had.

"They all miss you and hope you're having a good time with your sister," Kasey concluded.

"I am, child, I am! Ask Bessie. We are like two silly youngsters, laughing and crying and reminiscing. We are delighted to be together again."

"Kasey," Bessie interrupted, "would you like to help me serve the refreshments?"

"Sure." She looked at Olive. "I'll be right back."

"Take your time, child. I'm not going anywhere."

Kasey went to the kitchen where Bessie was filling glasses with ice cubes. She turned to Kasey and said confidentially, "I wanted to talk with you alone. Remember when you mentioned something about my sister's heart condition?"

"Heart condition?" Kasey stared at Bessie. "I said there was some talk of heart trouble, but I never knew what it was. Is it serious?"

"I am afraid so," said Bessie. "Olive's heart is not good. Not good at all. She had a spell the other evening. I called the paramedics. They took her to the hospital overnight. The doctor says it is congestive heart failure. She is better now, but it will get worse in time, and one day—poof—she will be gone."

"You mean—?" The words caught in Kasey's throat. "Are you saying—she doesn't have long to live?"

"I'm sorry, Kasey. I thought perhaps you knew. But Olive is very secretive—a very private person. Apparently she wanted no one to know. Please don't tell her I told you."

"I—I won't. I'm just so—surprised. And so sorry. You two just found each other."

"Yes, and I intend to care for Olive as long as I can. I have a health care nurse come in every day to check her. If Olive gets worse, I will see that she goes back to the hospital." Bessie handed Kasey a tray with cookies, plates, and napkins. "Take these out to the coffee table, and I will bring the drinks."

Kasey nodded and took out the tray. Bessie followed with iced tea and Cokes. Ryan was sitting on the sofa beside Olive, dutifully filling her in on the latest gossip from Shady Oaks. He looked relieved when the refreshments arrived, and happy that he could let someone else pick up the conversational ball.

Bessie was glad to oblige. She launched eagerly into stories of their childhood in Poland. "Olive and I were not close then. I was four years younger than she. I was a whiny, bothersome little nuisance. When Olive was nine she received a beautiful doll for her birthday. It had long blonde hair. None of us in our family had seen such golden tresses. We all had black hair. I was only five, but I was terribly jealous that Olive had such a beautiful blonde doll."

Olive chuckled. "Oh, you should have seen what this little scoundrel did."

"I am getting to that, dear sister," said Bessie. "So one day I took Olive's doll and dipped its long curls into the inkwell until they were all pitch black as night. And, oh, what a mess the doll was, with ink on its face and all over its frilly dress."

"It was a terrible sight." Olive scowled. "I cried for two days, and, oh, I vowed to get even with Bessie."

"Did you?"

"Yes. But I paid dearly for my revenge."

"What'd you do?" asked Ryan, between mouthfuls of cookies.

Olive's eyes gleamed. "I took Bessie's little lace petticoats and dipped them into the inkwell. Goodness, they looked ghastly!"

"Did your mom get mad?" asked Kasey.

"Oh, yes, she certainly did. She made me earn money and buy Bessie new petticoats. It took me six months.

My parents could easily have bought them, but they wanted me to learn the value of money."

"And respect for another's possessions," added Bessie, winking.

"Yes, little sister. I learned my lesson well."

"Our parents were very strict, but scrupulously fair," said Bessie. "I, too—even at five—had to do chores to pay for my sister's doll."

Olive smiled, her eyes lighting with once-forgotten memories. "Strangely enough, I came to love that doll with the ink-black hair. When my mother said I could have a new one, I said no, I loved the one I had, and if I got a new one perhaps I would not love her as much."

"But enough about us," said Bessie. "Tell me about your music, Kasey. Where did you learn to play so well?"

"I started taking piano lessons when I was five or six. It seems like I've been playing forever."

"I predict you will do great things with your music," said Bessie, sipping her tea. "Where do you plan to study?"

Kasey sighed a little and repeated the story of how she had always dreamed of studying at Juilliard. But now, with her father out of work, she would be attending the local junior college with Ryan and her brother.

"But what about your music?" persisted Bessie.

"I don't know," said Kasey. "I'll just have to leave it up to the Lord."

"Well, that is not something to leave to chance," scoffed Olive. "You must get the best training. Your talent demands it."

Kasey blinked away sudden tears. That was exactly the way she felt about it too, but what good did it do feeling that way when there just wasn't any money?

"What about scholarships?" asked Bessie.

"A few months ago I won a partial scholarship for $2,000 in the Springfield Piano Competition," said Kasey, "but I need ten times that much for just one year at Juilliard."

"There are other scholarships."

"I tried, but I was turned down."

"So are you saying you must be content with second best?" said Olive with a hint of indignation.

"Going to junior college isn't necessarily second best," protested Ryan. "Kasey has other things in her life besides music."

"Like a certain boy we all know?" mused Bessie.

Ryan ran his hand through his hair. "Yeah, you could say that."

"Do I hear wedding bells in your future?" Bessie asked merrily.

Ryan's face flushed, and Kasey squirmed uncomfortably.

When neither answered, Olive spoke up. "Don't be silly, sister dear. Kasey has her calling. She has no time for frivolous things like romance."

Kasey met Ryan's gaze. She could tell he was about ready to bolt for the door. "Actually, I do have time for romance," she corrected. "It's no secret. Ryan and I love each other."

"Ah," said Bessie, "that is quite another story. A wonderful love story!"

"Love is very nice," said Olive in her no-nonsense voice, "but do not let yourselves be tied down yet. In the next few years you will change a great deal. It will amaze you how much you change. Wait until then to see if you still want each other when you are different people."

Ryan stood up. "I don't care who Kasey is—now or four years from now. I love her, and I intend to marry her whenever she'll have me." Abruptly, he picked up the empty glasses and cookie platter and carried them to the kitchen.

Kasey stood up too and said nervously, "I guess we'd better go. We've got church tomorrow, and I've still got to wash my hair and all that stuff." She went over and kissed Olive's cheek and gave Bessie a quick hug. "Thanks for everything. It was great to see you both."

"Wait, I'll walk you to the door," said Bessie. When they were beyond Olive's hearing, she said, "I would like to come to your church sometime, but I cannot leave Olive. She is very hurt about my new faith. She does not understand that I still worship the God of Abraham, Isaac, and Jacob. I try to show her in the Jewish holy books, in the writings of Moses and David and Isaiah and Jeremiah, that Jesus is our Messiah who was prophesied, but she will not listen."

"I'll keep praying for her," said Kasey.

"Thank you, dear. My sister is a very stubborn lady, but don't worry. I am stubborn too."

Kasey paused in the doorway. "Have you talked about —you know—what happened in the concentration camps?"

Bessie's expression clouded. "No, dear. Those memories are too filled with darkness. They are too bitter for us to taste yet. One day the words will have to be spoken. But right now, in our joy at being together, we can speak only of fond memories—of our childhood, our parents, our brothers and sisters, our happy times before the soldiers came."

Kasey nodded. She didn't know what else to say, except "Thanks so much for having us over. We'll stop by again real soon."

Later, in the car on the way home, Ryan told Kasey, "I hope you didn't pay any attention to what those two said about waiting to get married. They're old ladies. What do they know about it?"

"But they did make sense, Ryan," she argued. "We will be different people when we're twenty-two. What if we don't like what the other's become? What if we're going in different directions? What if we don't want the same things out of life?"

Ryan's voice was edged with anger. "Well, Kase, if we wait till then to think about marriage, we're sure to be different people going different ways. The way I see it, we should get married young so we can grow up together and carve out one future for the two of us."

Kasey slunk down in her seat and kept her gaze focused on the road ahead. "I guess you're right." But privately she wondered, *Whose future will we be carving out? And what does God really want me to do?*

12

Every weekend during May, except one, Kasey went to visit Bessie Golden and Olive Solomon. Usually she went without Ryan because he had long since tired of "woman talk." But Kasey found the two women absolutely fascinating. They no longer avoided the subject of the Holocaust. Instead, they poured out their feelings with great bursts of emotion, so that sometimes, when they had finished, Kasey felt emotionally drained herself. But she would not have traded these days with Olive and Bessie for anything else in the world.

The one weekend that Kasey didn't visit the two sisters, she went instead to Middleton to see Dusty and her best friend, Diana Morley. Actually, she went for the fitting of her bridesmaid dress, but, more than that, she wanted to confirm in her mind that this improbable wedding was truly going to take place. Her own Dusty, whose friendship she treasured, was really going to marry her best friend!

Kasey was relieved to have Ryan drive her to Middleton. At least she wouldn't have to face Dusty and Diana alone. But, then again, Kasey knew Ryan had ulterior motives. He didn't trust Dusty, and in spite of Dusty's engagement Ryan didn't want Dusty spending even a minute alone with Kasey. But that was OK. With this whole new, unexpected change in their relationship, Kasey wasn't sure how to behave around Dusty anyway. For both Diana's and Ryan's sakes, she would have to practice thinking of Dusty in brotherly terms. Not easy to do when she still felt that quickening heartbeat in his presence.

Shortly after Kasey and Ryan arrived in Middleton and settled in at Grandma and Grandpa Carlone's farmhouse, Diana Morley came by and picked Kasey up in her red Mustang convertible. They drove to the bridal shop in the new mall just outside of town where Kasey got her first glimpse of the bridesmaid's dress she would be wearing.

"It's beautiful," she cried, her gaze sweeping over the pastel pink chiffon gown. "I'll feel like Cinderella in that!"

"Wait'll you see my wedding dress," said Diana. "It's totally awesome!" She disappeared into the dressing room and emerged minutes later in a flowing satin wedding gown adorned with sequins and lace.

"Oh, Diana, you're the most gorgeous bride I've ever seen!"

"Really? That's how I feel."

"Really and truly! You're absolutely radiant! I love it!" And it was true. Diana's face glowed, and her long blonde hair cascaded over her shoulders like a sun-washed waterfall. All evidence was gone of Diana's crack cocaine addiction last summer. She looked healthier and happier than Kasey had ever seen her.

On the drive back to Middleton, Kasey told Diana, "I'm really proud of you for the way you've gotten your life back together."

Diana nodded, her eyes on the road ahead. "Yeah, me too. I really went off the deep end last summer, huh? Hooked on crack. A common thief. Lying to everyone. I guess I really blew people away with all my stunts."

"Well, what's important is that you've straightened your life out. Everyone in town's pulling for you."

"I know that." Diana's voice wavered a little. "It wasn't easy, you know. Going through that drug rehab program. Getting off crack. I felt like I was going to die. I wanted to die. But I made it. And I know I'm lucky to be alive. I'll never get near that stuff again."

"I'm glad, Diana. You don't know how I worried about you, and how I prayed for you."

"That's what got me through, Kasey. Everyone's prayers."

Kasey looked curiously at Diana. "There's just one thing I don't understand."

"What's that?"

"You and Dusty. How did you two ever get together? You two had such a rocky history. You hated each other."

Diana laughed lightly. "Oh, boy! It's a long, long story."

"I've got time."

Diana looked at her. "You still care about him, don't you?"

"Dusty? Sure. We're friends. I hope we'll always be friends."

"But I know it was more than that, for both of you."

Kasey said seriously, "I'm in love with Ryan."

"I know. I can see it when you look at him. He's a doll. You two are great together."

"I think so. But you still haven't explained—"

"About Dusty. I know. It's totally crazy. I mean, I considered him this rude dude drifter, and he saw me as this spoiled little rich girl. Like you said, we hated each other."

"So how'd you go so fast from hate to love?"

"I'm getting to that. It was right after I got sent to the drug rehab center. Dusty started visiting me. I mean, it nearly blew me away. Most of my friends didn't want anything to do with me after I got in trouble. But Dusty—he was there for me."

"He's a pretty special guy," said Kasey.

"Yeah, he is. At first, I just shined him off, told him to take a hike. I didn't want anyone to know how I was hurting, especially a macho hunk like Dusty. I wanted to keep my glamour girl image. But Dusty saw through that. He wouldn't let me push him away. He didn't care how bad I looked or how awful I acted."

"He never told me any of this, Diana. I never realized—"

"I didn't want him to tell anyone. I didn't want people to know what I was going through. You know how it is, Kasey. The folks in Middleton are nice, ordinary farm people. Trusting and naive. They don't know about the dark side of life, what it's like to be involved with drugs and drug pushers. But Dusty understood. He's been knocked around all his life by people. He's seen everything. Nothing shocks him. And what's most important, Kasey"—Diana hesitated—"I don't know exactly how to say this—"

"What, Diana? Just say it."

"I'm not sure you'll understand."

"Try me."

"All right. The truth is, Dusty accepts me for who I am. He doesn't expect me to be a 'perfect little lady,' like my folks always wanted. He doesn't expect me to be a shining example, like you've always been, Kasey."

"Me? A shining example? You're kidding!"

"No, it's true. Everyone counts on you being a good girl, always doing the right thing, and you never disappoint them. But me—I'm not like that. I know I'm spoiled, stubborn, and self-centered. I'll never win any prizes for being a great humanitarian. And neither will Dusty. We're both just average people who have a knack for falling on our faces. But we're tough. And we're survivors."

"I don't think you're being fair to yourself, Diana—or to Dusty."

"Sure, I am, Kasey. Face it. We'll never have the lofty goals you and Ryan have—the grand ideals. We're not visionaries like you. Goodness, I wouldn't want to be."

Kasey laughed self-consciously. "You're not making any sense, Diana. Ryan and I aren't—"

"Wanna bet? Look at you two. You want to be a great concert pianist. And from what you said, Ryan wants to be a doctor, or a teacher, or a missionary to the poor people in Mexico or Timbuktu or who knows where. And you say you guys aren't idealistic dreamers?"

Kasey gazed out the window at the rolling countryside dotted with cozy farmhouses and weathered barns. "What's wrong with being a dreamer?" she asked.

"Nothing," said Diana quickly. "It's great for you. But it's not me—although I used to think it was. All my life I wanted to grow up and get out of Middleton and see what the rest of the world was like. I wanted to live high and experience everything. That's what I thought I was doing last summer when I zoned out on crack. But now I know better. Now I just want something solid and stable in my life. And that's what Dusty wants too."

"So it sounds like you guys know what you're getting into."

Diana smiled. "I hope so. But how about you and Ryan? When are you two going to take the plunge?"

"You mean get engaged? Married?"

"Sure, why not? You're in love, aren't you?"

"Yes, but—"

"Don't let him get away, Kasey. You may never find another guy like him."

Kasey nodded. It was true. She had already lost Dusty. She couldn't take a chance on losing Ryan.

"There are a lot of jerks out there," Diana continued as she turned onto the narrow, winding road that led to the Carlone farm. "Real losers, you know? But now that I've found my man, I'm not letting him get away!"

Kasey didn't reply. She looked at the familiar pastures and fields and remembered last summer with Dusty —the walks they had taken, the talks they'd had on her grandparents' screened front porch. Now Ryan was there waiting for her. He was probably chatting politely with Dusty, maintaining their uneasy truce and wondering why she and Diana were taking so long. Yes, Dusty belonged to Diana now, but Ryan was still hers—unless she happened to do something to drive him away.

"Oh, Kasey," Diana said brightly, "remind me to show you the brochures for our honeymoon trip. Would you believe? My folks are giving Dusty and me a cruise to the Bahamas. Imagine how romantic it will be!"

Later that evening, after Diana had gone home and Dusty had gone to his bunkhouse, Kasey and Ryan took a walk down by the creek. The crickets were chirping, and the air was cool and moist. Kasey loved the country smells of lilacs in bloom, rich black soil, and dew-wet grasses. Everything smelled new and fresh, as if the world had just been washed by a spring rain.

"Do you notice how different the country sounds from the city?" said Kasey as they stepped along the weedy shore bed to the creek.

"It sure sounds quieter," said Ryan. "No horns honking or cars screeching. But those crickets sound loud enough to be three-footers."

"They are," laughed Kasey. "We grow them big here in Middleton. Just wait'll you see one."

"No, thanks. I've already got a pet at home—a nice mongrel dog."

"Crickets are easier. You don't have to walk them." When they reached the creek, Kasey bent down and picked up a stone. She threw it out into the murky, moon-washed water. It made a distant little plopping sound. *Sloop!* She threw another pebble. "Watch, Ryan. You can see the frogs jumping. Listen. Do you hear them croaking? They all sound like they've got a frog in their throats."

"Funny," said Ryan, drawing her into his arms. "Hey, you're cold. Clammy, in fact. Maybe we'd better head back."

"In a minute," she murmured. She looked up at him. The moonlight glinted in his dark eyes and made a silhouette of his face. "I've always wanted to walk to this creek with the man I love, Ryan. When I was a little girl, I'd come here and dream about what it would be like to be grown up and love somebody, and I'd picture the two of us coming here and looking out at the water and talking about our future. And it would be like everything in my life had come full circle. Do you know what I mean?"

"I guess so. Like, you're not a kid anymore. You've changed, but the creek is still there like it always was."

"Right. And I even dream of coming back here someday when I have kids of my own and watching them play here and climb the trees I used to climb." She looked up at him. "I suppose I sound impossibly sentimental."

He bent his head and kissed her. "No, you sound terrific." He kissed her again. "And you taste wonderful too."

"Ryan," she whispered, "we need to talk."

"No, we talk too much. We're always talking." He took her hand and led her over to the grass and sat down.

She held back. "No, Ryan."

"What's wrong?"

"I'm afraid."

"There's nothing to be afraid of."

"Yes, there is."

"What? Bears, wolves, elephants? We're on a farm. There's nothing here but chickens and cows. What are you afraid of?"

"Us."

He pulled her down beside him. "You know me, Kase. I'd never hurt you. I just want us to be close."

"So do I, but—"

He wrapped her in his arms, and they sat like that for a long moment, neither saying a word, so close their hearts were beating as one. Kasey felt a panicky sensation in her chest as she remembered a moment like this last year, with Dusty. How close they had come to going too far. She couldn't let that happen with Ryan.

"We can't," she whispered.

"Why not?"

"You know."

"All I know is how much I want you."

"Me too—but it's wrong."

"Right now it feels so right."

Kasey wriggled away. "No, Ryan. God doesn't want this for us!"

"How do you know?"

"I know—and you know too." She stood up, breathless. "Come on, we'd better get back. I'm cold."

She started walking, and he caught up with her and clasped her hand. "I'm sorry," he said. "I wouldn't have done it—you know—"

"Are you sure?"

"It's just—sometimes when we're together I get a little crazy. I wish—I wish we were like Dusty and Diana—getting married this June. Then being together would be right."

Kasey nodded. "Sometimes it's what I want too. Other times the idea petrifies me. I hate feeling so confused. Is it always going to be like this—being too young, wanting something we can't have, not knowing what God wants for us? I feel like I'm going to be seventeen forever."

"Same here." Ryan's voice was edged with frustration. "It's not like I don't pray about it. I do. All the time. I keep telling God I just want His will. And in a way, it's true. But in another way—" He paused, and his tone grew solemn. "The truth is, I want what I want—and that's you, Kasey, no matter what God says. Do you think He'll punish me for feeling that way?"

Kasey stopped and looked at Ryan. They were only a few yards from the farmhouse now. "Ryan, God wants what's best for us. He's not playing games with us."

"Then why do I feel like I'm being jerked around all the time?"

"Because that's how life is. Part of us wants what's right, and part of us wants what's wrong. It's like a war."

He grimaced. "Well, I'm battle-weary already." He reached out and nudged her chin. "Something's got to give, Kasey. You see that, don't you?"

She stared up at him. "No. What do you mean?"

"I mean, I can't keep up this emotional roller-coaster indefinitely. Neither of us can. Things will go one way or another."

"What way?"

"We'll either get closer—or we'll drift apart. Things don't remain static."

She said the words in a little sob. "I don't want us to drift apart, Ryan."

"Then let's get engaged."

The words took her by surprise, but she instinctively shook her head. "I don't know. Is it what God wants?"

"If it isn't, He'll stop us. Come on. How about it? Just say yes!"

"I don't want to do it this way, Ryan. I want to be sure first."

"Listen, Kase. At least say we can be engaged to be engaged. Then, if it's still right when we graduate in June, we can tell the whole world. OK?"

She drew in a deep breath. "I—I guess that would be OK. But if I feel it's not right when graduation comes—if I don't want to be engaged—we'll just forget it and not tell anyone, OK?"

He swung her up in his arms and kissed her hard on the lips. "Deal! But I've got a feeling, Kase. We were meant to be together. You wait and see. Our love will last forever!"

13

That night, Kasey settled into the pretty blue room she always occupied when staying at her grandparents' house, the same sunny room she had stayed in last summer. But she knew even as she slipped into her pajamas that she wasn't the least bit sleepy. Only an hour ago she had practically told Ryan they could consider themselves engaged. But now the very idea struck her with waves of terror.

She sat down cross-legged on the bed and hugged her floppy old Winnie the Pooh against her chest. She always kept him on her bed and even carried him in her overnight bag when she spent the night away from home. Except for sleep-overs at Selena's or Jenny's or Diana's. Her Pooh bear wasn't something she wanted her friends to know about. They were much too sophisticated for Pooh. Or were they?

Kasey wondered whimsically, *If I marry Ryan, will he let me take Pooh Bear to bed with me? Will I want to?* It was all too incongruous, too absurd to imagine. How could it be that one moment she wanted desperately to sleep with Ryan and the next moment she wanted only to cuddle up with her old stuffed bear?

"Lord Jesus," she said aloud, softly, so that no one could hear, "we need to talk. I mean, really talk." She pulled distractedly at the tufts on her bedspread, mulling over what she wanted to say. "You know how much I want to be with Ryan. Please let it work out. Let him be the one for me." She paused, then after a long moment added, "But even more than I want Ryan, I want Your will. So help me be strong and do what's right—and help me to know what to do."

As Kasey finished praying, she was already starting to feel deliciously sleepy, so she stretched and yawned, then turned off the light and climbed under the covers, and snuggled up with Pooh in her arms.

On Sunday morning, Grandma Carlone served a big breakfast of hot cakes, scrambled eggs, and Italian sausage, and insisted that Ryan have seconds, then thirds—Grams's way of making a visitor feel welcome and cared for. After breakfast, Kasey and Ryan attended church with her grandparents, although they ended up sitting with Dusty and Diana. After church, they packed up their things and headed back for Springfield. It was a four-hour drive, and Ryan had promised Kasey's mother he'd have her home before dark—and in time for the evening service at Community Bible.

They made the drive without incident, stopping only for a tank of gas and a couple of burgers, and arrived at Kasey's house on Wildwood Drive shortly after 5:00 P.M.

"Over an hour to spare before church," Ryan told Kasey as they walked through the foyer to the living room.

"We're home!" Kasey called out. "Where's everyone?"

"Upstairs getting ready," her mother called back. "There's a note for you on the fridge. Sounds important."

Kasey beckoned Ryan toward the kitchen. "Come on. Let's check the fridge."

"Great. Now that you mention it, I'm starved."

"I'm not talking food," she teased. "I've got a message."

She took the note off the refrigerator and scanned it quickly, feeling a wave of alarm ripple through her. "Listen to this. Bessie Golden called. She says Olive's in the hospital, and she's there with her. What could have happened?"

"Doesn't she say?"

"No. Just that I can call her at this number."

"Well, go ahead."

Kasey reached for the phone and dialed, then asked the operator for Olive Solomon's room. After a minute, Bessie came on the line.

"Bessie? This is Kasey Carlone. I just got home and got your message. What happened to Olive?"

Bessie sighed heavily. "Oh, dear girl, it's her heart. I thought we were going to lose her. She's better now. Stable, they say. But, oh, she gave me a scare!"

"Can I come see her?"

"Oh, I was hoping you would. You will perk up her spirits with your smile. I just know it."

Kasey looked at Ryan. "Will you drive me?"

"Sure. Come on. Maybe we can still make it to church afterwards."

They arrived at Springfield General Hospital fifteen minutes later and walked down the long hallway to the cardiac care unit. Ryan waited outside while Kasey went in and stole quietly over to Olive Solomon's bed. Bessie was standing there, rubbing Olive's arm gently and murmuring soothing words in Polish. She smiled with tearful eyes when she saw Kasey. "Dear girl, I am so glad to see you. Come close so Olive can see you."

Kasey approached the bedside with trepidation, not knowing what she would find. The sight made her flinch. That proud, aristocratic lady Kasey loved was now a frail, gray figure tied to machines and tubes. Her once sparkling eyes were clouded and vague. Her expressive face sagged with exhaustion. The Olive Solomon Kasey knew and adored was gone.

Kasey looked quickly at Bessie. "Will she get better?"

"I hope so. I trust God for her life. I believe He will not let her go until she knows Him."

Kasey leaned over the bed and gazed directly into Olive's eyes. "Olive, can you hear me? It's me, Kasey. How are you?"

"How do you think I am?" Olive whispered back hoarsely. "How would you be, stuck all over with needles and pins?"

Kasey chuckled in spite of herself. So Olive had retained her rare sense of humor! Surely she would be all right after all.

For two days Olive remained in the cardiac care unit. Then, when her condition improved, she was transferred to a private room. That evening, when Kasey stopped by to see her, Olive was sitting up in bed eating a cup of custard. Bessie hovered beside her, fretting and fluttering like a mother bird.

Olive beamed when she spotted Kasey. But as Kasey approached her bedside, she noticed that Olive looked many years older. The wrinkles in her face had deepened into crevices, and her eyes were shadowed with weariness. Her complexion was an eerie mottled gray.

"Well, look at you!" said Kasey, a little too brightly. "You're sure looking better than you did a couple days ago." True enough, but the greater truth was that Olive had failed immeasurably. Silently Kasey prayed that Olive wouldn't see the shock and distress in her eyes.

Olive stretched out a feeble hand toward Kasey's. "I tell them I am well enough to go home with Bessie, but they will not listen to me. They are stubborn mules, these doctors."

"Now, now, sister," said Bessie, "you have very good doctors."

"Perhaps, but I am bored here. There is nothing to do but wait for nurses to poke and prod me, and lie here watching game shows on TV."

"You like game shows," said Bessie.

"I do not," said Olive stubbornly. "I tolerate them—as I tolerate the nurses who wake me up to give me a pill to sleep."

Bessie looked bemusedly at Kasey. "She is getting better, don't you think?"

"Oh, absolutely. I can tell by her good humor."

Olive folded her frail arms in a gesture of defiance. "I will be in good humor when they tell me I can go home."

Kasey looked over and noticed a Bible sitting on the bedstand. She looked questioningly at Bessie.

"I have been reading Olive the Holy Scriptures," she said matter of factly, stifling a smile. "She loves the Psalms of David."

"Is that so, Mrs. Solomon?" Kasey asked in surprise. "You like the Psalms?"

Olive lifted her chin proudly. "Is that so strange, child? We Jews had the Psalms long before you Christians. Even your Jesus is a Jew, you know."

"I know," said Kasey. "I know the whole story. The Jews are God's chosen people. And you have been watching for your Messiah for many, many centuries. And since

I accepted the Lord Jesus as my Messiah, I feel sort of like an adopted Jew."

Olive didn't reply right away. Kasey could see that she was rolling the idea around in her mind, trying it on for size, deciding whether to be offended or amused. Finally she looked up at Kasey and smiled. "I would certainly adopt you into my family, child. Your heart is good and pure. It is love like yours that will defeat the hatred of those who seek to destroy us."

"Destroy you? You mean the Nazis during the war? But that ended nearly fifty years ago."

"The war is over, but the battle never ends," said Bessie.

"What do you mean?" asked Kasey.

"I mean there are many who spread lies about us even today, wicked people who claim that the Holocaust did not exist, that Jews did not die. They seek to rewrite the history books and make people forget the horrors and obscenities of the death camps."

"But people will never forget. How could they?"

"It is human nature to forget what is not buried deep within the heart," said Bessie. "But for most people in this world today, it is not simply a matter of forgetting. They do not know about the death camps. Many have never heard. Some who hear do not believe. They know only what survivors tell them. And soon there will be no survivors. Who will tell people then? And who will keep it from happening again?"

Kasey chewed solemnly on her lower lip. She couldn't imagine such atrocities happening again in a world that had lived through such pain and misfortune. And yet she had heard tales of similar tragedies in Cambodia and other countries around the world. And what about the millions of abortions performed right in her own country? Weren't they a holocaust of sorts?

Impulsively Kasey leaned over Olive's bed and kissed her gently on the forehead. "Here's one who will never forget," she promised. "I will always carry you in my heart."

14

When Kasey visited the hospital the following weekend, she was startled to find Olive Solomon's room empty. "Where is Olive?" she quickly asked a passing nurse.

"Oh, I think she and her sister are in the sun room. Just down the hall and to your right."

The sun room? Did that mean Olive was feeling well enough to be up and around? Kasey hurried down the hall, nearly running, her shoes clattering on the tile floor. Sure enough, she found Olive sitting in a wheelchair by the plate glass windows, looking out at the sprawling, sun-spangled city. Bessie was sitting on the sofa beside her, working on her needlepoint.

Kasey was breathless as she greeted the two sisters. "Boy, I was worried," she told Olive, sitting down beside her. "You weren't in your room. But here you are traipsing around the hospital and looking wonderful."

"I am even better now that you are here, child," said Olive, reaching out a tentative hand to Kasey.

"Like they say, you cannot keep a good woman down," said Bessie.

"Does this mean you'll go home soon?" asked Kasey.

"I hope so. I am tired of hospital life. The food is too bland, and the nurses are too cheerful, even when they are sticking a needle in me. I want to be back home with Bessie."

"Well, you're looking so good," said Kasey. "Your cheeks even have some color in them. That's a good sign."

Olive patted Kasey's hand and smiled. "You tell the doctors you have made your diagnosis. I am well and ready to go home."

"I sure will. Let me at 'em."

"You look happy and full of energy," noted Olive, looking Kasey over. "Is your life as busy as ever?"

"Busier. I'm swamped with term papers and tests and piano recitals and final projects. It's just six weeks till graduation, and I feel like I'm running in every direction at once."

"And still you have time to come here and gossip with two old ladies," said Olive.

"What about that boyfriend of yours?" asked Bessie. "Are you still finding time for him?"

"Trying to." Kasey didn't dare mention that she and Ryan were still going in circles about getting engaged. No one else knew they were even considering such a thing. "He's busy too, working lots of hours and trying to keep up his grades."

"He's graduating too, isn't he?" said Bessie.

"Right. He'll be going to Springfield Community College next year."

"And have you decided yet where you will be going?" asked Olive.

Kasey fidgeted a little, weighing her words. "I—I'll probably be going to Springfield Community too."

"But what about Juilliard? I thought you were accepted there."

"I was—but I withdrew my application."

Olive looked up in surprise. "Why, child?"

"Uh, it's too expensive," Kasey said uneasily. "And my dad's still out of work."

"But you owe it to your talent to go to Juilliard," protested Olive. "It is your destiny. It will determine whether you are to be a great artist or a mediocre one."

"Olive, please," said Bessie. "Don't be so rigid, so inflexible. I am sure Kasey will do well wherever she studies."

"I am not being rigid. I am being honest."

"But you make her feel bad because she cannot go to Juilliard."

"It's OK," said Kasey. "I'm getting used to the idea of staying in Springfield. I'll be with all my friends next year—Jenny and Selena and, of course, Ryan. In fact, Ryan and I—" She let her words drift off, lest she say more than she intended.

"What about Ryan and you?" asked Olive. "Is there more you are not telling us?"

Kasey felt her face grow warm. "Not exactly. It's just—"

"Ah," said Bessie with a knowing smile, "are we to hear wedding bells sometime soon?"

"Don't be silly, sister," said Olive. "Kasey is much too young to think of marriage."

"Actually, I am thinking about it," Kasey admitted. "At least, Ryan and I have talked about it. But that's all."

"Well, talk is cheap," said Olive. "As long as you only talk about it."

"Ryan is a very nice boy," said Bessie. "Look how he visits Shady Oaks every week. He is a very caring young man. There are not many left like him."

Kasey nodded. "He's the most wonderful boy I've ever known."

"So, you are truly in love!" said Olive, her eyes narrowing.

"I think so," said Kasey, feeling suddenly shy and tongue-tied. Trying to know what was or was not love was like exploring unknown terrain. Foreign territory. Alien spheres. Just when she thought she had it all figured out, she discovered some new facet of it that left her feeling uncertain and confused again. How did anyone know for sure that she was in love and not merely "in like"? And if it was truly love, how could one be sure it was God's will and not merely her own desires?

"Well, sister," said Bessie, "I think by Kasey's expression that we are on the verge of meddling. Perhaps we should stifle our inquisitiveness."

"No, that's OK," said Kasey. "My mind just wandered for a minute. What were you saying?"

"We are saying only that we want the best for you, child. God's very best for you."

"Thanks." Kasey sat forward and glanced at her watch. "I suppose I should be going. I've got a ton of homework to do and an hour of piano practice tonight."

Bessie spoke up. "Wait, Kasey. I think Olive has something to tell you. Don't you, sister?"

Kasey looked at Olive. "Is that right? A problem?"

"Oh, no, no," scoffed Olive. "Life is very good to me right now."

"Then what?"

"Tell her, Olive," prompted Bessie. "It is what we have prayed for, dear child."

Kasey's heart skipped a beat. "You mean—?"

"Yes. This is a time for joy. Tell her, sister."

"I am getting to it," said Olive. "It is not easy to find the words."

"What words? What? Tell me!" urged Kasey excitedly.

"Very well." Olive took both Kasey's hands in hers and clasped them against her paper-thin cheeks. Tears moistened her dark eyes. Her voice was throaty, emotion-filled. "It is simply this. I am no more a stranger to this Jesus of yours. He is now my friend and my redeemer also."

"Oh, Mrs. Solomon—!"

"That makes us sisters, little one, for we are children of the same heavenly Father."

Kasey bent over the wheelchair and circled Olive's frail body in her arms. She couldn't keep back the tears. "I am so happy—!"

"It is because you opened the door, child, and made me look outside myself, beyond my bitterness and anger. You made me remember what love looks like. You kept on loving me until my heart became tender enough to let your Jesus inside. For that I thank you with all my heart, little one."

"Oh, but thank Bessie too," said Kasey. "She talked to you over and over about her faith and read the Scriptures to you every day. She's responsible too!"

"Yes, she is," Olive agreed, "but don't you see, child? If you had not already made my heart tender, I would have rejected Bessie's faith. I would have resisted her words. I would have closed my heart and mind to her prayers."

"It's true," said Bessie. "Only I know how stubborn my sister can be. God has indeed worked a miracle in her life."

"But I am still every bit a Jew," declared Olive, her black eyes twinkling. "Only now I know that my Messiah lives."

15

On Monday evening Bessie telephoned Kasey to tell her that Olive had been released from the hospital. "We took a taxi home, and I am getting her settled in. We will have a visiting nurse check on her every other day."

"Then Olive's feeling well?" asked Kasey.

"Oh, yes, as spirited and feisty as ever. In fact, we would like you to come to dinner one night soon. And bring Ryan, of course. It will be something simple. Goulash or salmon loaf. But then I suppose you would rather have cheeseburgers or tacos."

"Oh, anything's fine, but I'll have to take a raincheck. These next few days are jam-packed."

"I understand. Call us when you are free, and we will plan something."

"Great! Give Olive my love. Bye-bye."

As soon as Kasey hung up the phone, it rang again. It was Ryan.

"Just wanted to make sure we're still on for tonight."

"For sure," she said. "I want to get to the mall by seven. When can you pick me up?"

"A half hour. Just have to gobble down some dinner, and I'm on my way."

"Super." She was about to tell him about Olive coming home from the hospital but decided to wait until they were on their way to the mall. With all she had to do, every minute counted. "Hurry, Ryan," she said.

Twenty minutes later Ryan pulled into the Carlone driveway. Kasey called good-bye to her mother and ran out to meet him before he was even out of the car.

"Man, you are in a hurry," he said as she climbed in and buckled her seatbelt.

"I know. I've got to buy satin shoes for Diana's wedding and get them dyed the exact same color as my dress. I just got the swatch from Diana in the mail, so now I know the right color. And I've got to get white shoes to wear with my cap and gown. Heels, but not real high, so I don't fall on my face in front of everyone during the ceremony. And I have to pick up my graduation pictures at the photographer's so we can send them to everyone with my graduation announcements. Oh, that's right. I've got to pick up my announcements at the printer's!" She stopped, breathless, and leaned back against the headrest. "Oh, Ryan, I'll never make it! I'll never survive the wedding and graduation and—"

Ryan reached over and squeezed her knee. "Hey, get a grip, Kase. You won't make it coming unglued like this. Take a breath and relax."

She breathed in deeply, then exhaled. "OK, I'm hanging in there—but just barely." She looked over at him. "How come you're not tripping out over all you've got to do? We're in the home stretch, Ryan. Everything depends on these next few weeks."

He chuckled. "I guess I'm not as high-strung as you. But in my own way I'm panicky too. My grades are on the line. A lot's at stake. I'm plenty stressed out."

"At least you don't show it. I'm climbing the walls at home. Keith says I'm totally unhinged. Of course, he's mildly deranged himself. And my folks are still upset. Dad hasn't found a job. All he talks about is starting his own Mini-Mart, and here we're nearly broke. I told him he could use the money I earned from my TV show last fall, but he won't touch it. He might as well use it though. There's not enough for college. Actually, there's—"

"Hey, slow down," said Ryan. "You're talking faster than I'm driving."

"I'm sorry. See what I mean?" She looked out the window. They were heading down the main thoroughfare toward the mall.

"It's OK," said Ryan, chuckling. "It's just that you're wound so tight, you'll explode. And that wouldn't be a pretty sight."

"I just thought of something else," said Kasey. "Olive Solomon is out of the hospital. She's back home with her sister, and they want us to come to dinner sometime soon."

"I hope she's fixing something normal like cheeseburgers and not that weird stuff."

"It doesn't matter, Ryan. I told her we'd take a raincheck. We just have too much to do, with finals and graduation and Diana's wedding and all."

For the next two weeks Kasey was so caught up in schoolwork, piano recitals, and preparations for graduation and Diana's wedding that she had no time to stop by Bessie's to see Olive. But she telephoned every few days and chatted with the two sisters and was relieved to hear that Olive was growing stronger.

"I promise, next weekend—Friday or Saturday night—Ryan and I will come to visit," she assured Bessie. "How about if we bring in Kentucky Fried Chicken? That way you won't have to cook."

"We will look forward to seeing you, dear girl. Olive has missed you. And she misses all of her friends from Shady Oaks."

"We could drive her over sometime to see them," Kasey offered.

"Oh, no, child. Olive is still too weak to go out. But perhaps one day soon—"

"I have an idea," said Kasey. "You have Olive ready for guests on Friday night, and we'll bring the dinner, OK? We'll see you about six."

"Very well, Kasey. We will see you then."

As soon as Kasey hung up from Bessie, she telephoned Ryan. "Listen," she said with mounting excitement, "I've got this sensational idea. How about if we pick up some of the folks from Shady Oaks in your car and take them to visit Olive and Bessie?"

Ryan liked the idea. So on Friday night they picked up Mrs. Smolin, Mr. Suttles, Mrs. Pinkelman, and Mrs. Tisdale and drove them over to Bessie's apartment. While Kasey got the old-timers settled inside, Ryan drove to Kentucky Chicken and came back with potato salad, biscuits, and three buckets of steaming, crispy chicken. Bessie served tea and coffee, fluttering from guest to guest to make sure everyone was well satisfied.

Kasey knew that the happiest person of all tonight was Olive Solomon. She sat on the sofa with her afghan over her lap, eagerly drinking in all the conversations going on around her. Olive was too weak to say much, and she looked thinner than Kasey remembered, but her eyes were bright and filled with pure joy. All of the oldsters remarked about the change in Olive's countenance. This woman who had once been so solemn and subdued, even despondent, now practically glowed.

When her friends questioned Olive about her surprisingly sunny demeanor after all she'd just been through, she only smiled cryptically and murmured, "God is good. God is very good."

Later that evening, after returning the residents to Shady Oaks, Ryan drove Kasey home. The car still smelled faintly of chicken and Mrs. Pinkelman's lavender cologne. And in her mind Kasey could still hear Olive Solomon's gentle laughter as she bade her guests good night.

"Know what, Ryan?" said Kasey softly. "We did good tonight. We made some neat people real happy."

"We sure did."

"I feel pretty happy myself."

"Me too. I could do good stuff like this for a lifetime. I get a real charge out of it."

She looked over at him. "I guess that's why you want to be a doctor, or a teacher, or missionary, huh? So you can help people?"

"Guess so." Ryan's voice grew serious. "Actually, lately I've been thinking more about being a missionary than anything else. How about you?"

"What about me?"

"You like to help people. Do you ever think about being a missionary? You know, going to places like Mexico City, like we did last Christmas? Working full-time with poor people, sick people?"

Kasey shrugged. "I don't know. I love helping people—you know that. But I don't think of it as a career, like you do. It's just something I enjoy doing. When I think of something I want to dedicate my whole life to, I think of my music. I want to reach people through music, make them feel what I feel when I play. I guess that's different than what you want."

"But that doesn't mean we can't combine our goals—work together, serve the Lord together." He pulled into her driveway and turned off the engine. As he drew her into his arms, he whispered, "We're meant to be together, Kasey, and I'm going to pray that God will convince you of that."

"I'm praying about it, too, Ryan," she whispered back. "I love being with you. I feel so warm and safe and protected in your arms."

He kissed her tenderly. "Give me a chance, Kasey, and I'll take care of you for the rest of your life."

In the week that followed, Kasey thought a lot about what Ryan had said. *I'll take care of you for the rest of your life . . . take care of you . . . take care of you . . .* It sounded so good. So right. Certainly Ryan was the perfect boy for her—thoughtful, considerate, ambitious, sincere, a wonderful Christian who loved the Lord.

Why, then, didn't she feel peace about getting engaged? What was holding her back, keeping her from making a commitment? Why was she so afraid? And what was she going to tell Ryan when he was ready to put a ring on her finger? He had told her they would announce their engagement at graduation. Surely she would know her own heart by then.

One week after the impromptu chicken party at Bessie's apartment, Kasey received a frightening call. A woman's voice broke through a sob of emotion and said, "Kasey, you must come. Come at once!"

For a moment Kasey didn't recognize the voice. Then she knew. It was Bessie. "Bessie, what's wrong? Come where?"

"To the hospital. Hurry!"

"The hospital? What happened?"

Bessie's voice was tremulous, her words halting and confused. "I tried to help her—I tried. But it was too hard for me. I called on the telephone—the operator. I called that number—9-1-1. They sent the ambulance. Come quickly, Kasey. Olive needs you."

Kasey's mind raced, hungry for more information. What about Olive? What was wrong? But there was no time to pump Bessie for answers now. "I'll be right there," she promised. "I'll borrow my brother's car, or have my dad drive me. What room is she in?"

"The intensive care unit," said Bessie breathlessly. "Hurry!"

Kasey was too upset to drive herself, so she asked her dad to drive her to Springfield General. He pushed the speed limit and pulled up to the entrance doors in just ten minutes.

"Go on in," he told Kasey. "I'll park the car and wait for you in the lobby."

With her heart pounding in her ears, Kasey took the elevator up to the third floor, then nearly vaulted down the long hallway to the double doors of the intensive care unit. With her mouth dry as sandpaper, she approached the nurse at the desk and asked, "Where's Olive Solomon? I've got to see her."

"Are you family?" asked the nurse.

"Uh—no—not exactly. But we're friends. Good friends."

"I'm sorry. Only family is allowed."

Kasey's anger flared, but she managed to ask politely, "Will Olive be OK? She will be OK, right?"

"I'm sorry, miss. You'll have to speak to her doctor."

Just as Kasey was about to lose it, Bessie appeared from a little cubicle and bustled over. "At last, dear girl, you're here! Come! Olive wants to see you!"

"Wait," said the nurse. "Only family is allowed in there."

Bessie bristled indignantly and announced, "This is family. We are one in the family of God!"

While the nurse stared back in mute perplexity, Bessie ushered Kasey into the little cubicle. Kasey stared in dismay at the fragile figure in the hospital bed. It was Olive, all right, but she looked so pale and defenseless amid all the wires and tubes and machines. One ominous contraption made a beeping sound and showed the rhythm of Olive's heartbeat.

Kasey looked urgently at Bessie. "What happened?"

Bessie wept softly. "They think it was a massive heart attack. They make no promises . . ."

Kasey squeezed Bessie's hand. "She'll be all right. I promise."

A small, feeble voice whispered, "Kasey? Is that you?"

Kasey went over to the bed and gently placed her hand on Olive's cheek. Her skin felt as smooth as velvet, as delicate as ashes left by flames. "I'm here, Mrs. Solomon. How are you?"

"Better," she murmured. Her eyes remained distant, unseeing.

Kasey blinked back tears. "You're going to be fine. And we'll all come back for another party. We'll bring everyone over, like before, and we'll get buckets of chicken—"

"Good-bye, Kasey."

Kasey took Olive's hand and pressed it against her cheek. "Don't say good-bye. Don't ever say good-bye!"

The voice was wispy, hardly there. "Hello, then, little one."

The nurse stepped breezily into the cubicle and announced, "I'm sorry. You'll have to go now."

"But I just got here," Kasey protested.

"You're allowed five minutes every hour, miss. I'm sorry. Your time is up."

Kasey held fast to Olive's hand. "Just one more minute, please."

The nurse hesitated. "I've already stretched the rules, letting two visitors in at once."

"Oh, I'll step outside a minute," said Bessie quickly.

"Very well." The nurse cast another warning glance at Kasey and left.

"Mrs. Solomon? Can you hear me?" Kasey asked, bending close to her wrinkled, weathered face.

Olive's eyes opened and focused for just a moment on Kasey. "You gave me—a new song," she rasped. "Thank you." And then, as fleetingly as her eyes had opened, they closed.

"Mrs. Solomon? I love you," Kasey whispered. "You'll be fine, I know you will. Don't die. Please don't die!"

But even as Kasey rode home with her father later that evening, she knew deep inside that she would not see Olive Solomon again. It wasn't a conscious knowledge but rather a profound sadness that seeped into every corner of her soul and left her chilled to the very marrow of her bones. Never had she felt so numbingly cold before.

When the call came shortly after midnight, Kasey knew it would be Bessie with the news. She steeled herself, nearly shutting her ears to the terrible truth she already guessed. But the words came anyway, and nothing could have prepared Kasey for the stunning jolt that left her senses reeling.

"Olive is gone, dear girl. Our Olive has gone home to heaven."

16

They gathered for a graveside ceremony at a little country cemetery just outside Springfield—the handful of people who had loved Olive Solomon. Kasey's family was there, and the young people who had visited often at the retirement home, and Clarisa Huckabey and the residents of Shady Oaks. Bessie stood beside the closed casket while Kasey's pastor, John Shaw, a tall, strapping man with gentle eyes and a warm smile, prayed and read from the Scriptures.

"Mrs. Solomon's favorite book of the Bible was Isaiah," he said in his strong, bell-clear voice. "Of any books written under the law, Isaiah most clearly gives us a picture of grace. Olive Solomon was a woman who lived under the law, but in her final days she discovered the miracle of grace. She believed these verses in Isaiah nine were written especially for her. 'The people that walked in darkness have seen a great light; they that dwell in the land of the shadow of death, upon them hath the light shined. . . . For unto us a child is born, unto us a son is given, and the government shall be upon his shoulder; and his name shall be called Wonderful, Counselor, the Mighty God, the Everlasting Father, the Prince of Peace.'

"Olive Solomon knew the darkest shadows of death any human being can experience," continued Pastor Shaw. "She lost every member of her family, except her beloved sister, to the Nazi death camps, and she barely escaped with her own life. But she also came to know peace and the great joy of her Messiah's love and redemption. So let us rejoice with Olive in so great a salvation that can lift us from the darkest night of despair to the great saving light of Christ that shines upon all those who trust in Him! And let us remember with Isaiah that 'He will swallow up death in victory; and the Lord God will wipe away tears from all faces.'"

Everyone agreed after the service that it was one of the most beautiful, heart-stirring moments they had ever experienced. Many wept silently; others gazed in reflection at the cloudless, early morning sky. As everyone watched, Bessie placed a simple bouquet of daisies on the casket, explaining, "Olive loved daisies when she was a child. She loved spring flowers. But this is not a bouquet of goodbyes for my sister. It is a bouquet of new beginnings."

As people filed by the casket to pay their last respects, Bessie hugged each one and thanked them for coming. When it was Kasey's turn to greet Bessie, the two went into each other's arms and embraced for a long moment, weeping.

"I loved her so much," Kasey whispered, "like she was my own grandmother."

"I know, dear girl, and you were like a daughter to her. The daughter she never had." Bessie released Kasey and stepped back a little. She took Kasey's face in her hands and looked directly into her eyes. "Do not grieve long, little one. We must remember that Olive is happy at last. I am sure she is already singing one of her favorite arias for St. Peter. She will give heaven her own little taste of class."

Kasey smiled in spite of herself. "I'll try to think of her that way, Bessie, singing her new song in heaven. Singing for Jesus."

"That is what she would want, dear girl, that you remember her with joy, not with sadness." Bessie reached over and plucked a handful of daisies from the bouquet on the casket and gave them to Kasey. "For you. Press them in your Bible. Keep them, along with the memories of Olive tucked in your heart. May they remind you of all the beautiful things God has given us, and ease the pain you feel."

"I will," Kasey promised. "I'll keep them always."

But the days that followed Olive's funeral proved more difficult for Kasey than she ever would have dreamed. She found herself brooding frequently and feeling depressed. Dark, terrifying thoughts loomed up in her consciousness and left her feeling shaken, exhausted. *If Olive could die, what about my own mom and dad? What about Grandma and Grandpa Carlone? What about Keith or Ryan? What about me?*

Her mother noticed Kasey's gloom and commented on it one evening nearly a week after Olive's death. She had just said good night to Kasey when she paused in the doorway and asked, "Are you OK, honey? You've been looking pretty forlorn lately."

"You know why, Mom."

Her mother came over and sat down on the bed. Carefully she straightened the covers the way she had when Kasey was a child. "I know it hurts to lose someone you love," she said softly, "but I have this feeling there's something more."

Kasey looked away. "I can't explain it, Mom. I just feel weepy all the time. I—I never knew anyone who died before."

Her mother smoothed the sheet with long, tapered fingers. "It is hard. Death is always a shock. No matter how much we realize it's inevitable, we still don't expect it."

With sudden urgency Kasey searched her mother's eyes. "I don't get it, Mom. Olive was such a strong woman. She'd been through so much and survived. She seemed ageless, like she could just go on forever. I can't believe all that energy and talent and liveliness is just gone, so quickly, so finally."

Her mother put her cool hand on Kasey's forehead and brushed back her hair. "Olive is gone from us, but all that talent and energy are still very much alive."

Kasey nodded. "Right. In heaven. I know. But right now heaven seems so far removed, so unreal compared with a cold, stiff body being buried in the ground." Kasey's voice turned into a sob. "I never went to a funeral before, never saw anyone dead. Mom, if it ever happened to you or Dad, I couldn't stand it. I'd die."

Her mother took her in her arms. "No, you wouldn't die. God would see you through it, just like He'll see you through this."

"But how? I don't even understand what I'm feeling. Everything in my life is up for grabs right now. I just feel paralyzed, terrified."

Her mother looked closely at her. "Are some of these feelings about something else, Kasey? Like graduation? Or about college next year?"

"It's about everything, Mom," Kasey cried. "Olive is dead and I'm alive, and I don't even know who I am or what I'm supposed to do with my life!"

"Honey, God doesn't expect you to know the future or even to understand all your feelings. He only asks you to trust and obey Him today, this hour, and leave the rest to Him. He'll work it out, I know."

They hugged again, and Kasey brushed away her tears. "Thanks, Mom. I feel better. Good night."

And it was true. Kasey did feel better. But she felt something else she had never felt before—a sense of wanting to hold tight to the people she loved lest they, too, be snatched from her arms. Her parents, Ryan, even her brother, Keith. It occurred to her that she had lost Dusty and now Olive. She could not afford to lose anyone else she loved. Even the idea of marrying Ryan took on new appeal. Why not settle down and get married and worry about college later? After all, that's what Dusty and Diana were doing.

Three days before Diana and Dusty's wedding, Kasey received a strange phone call from a man who identified himself as Stuart Jenkins, an attorney at law. "Miss Kassandra Carlone," he said in a deep, formal voice, "I'm the attorney for Olive Solomon's estate, and I'm calling to advise you of a meeting at my office tomorrow morning at ten sharp."

"A meeting? What for?"

"For the reading of Mrs. Solomon's will."

"Oh, I don't think I'll be able to come, Mr. Jenkins," said Kasey. "We start finals next week, and I'm really busy. But thanks anyway."

"I'm sorry, Miss Carlone. You don't understand. It's imperative that you attend this meeting. In fact, I suggest that you bring your parents with you."

Kasey hesitated. "I guess we can be there, Mr. Jenkins, if you're sure it's important."

"Yes, Miss Carlone. I assure you it is important."

The next morning, as Kasey rode with her parents to the lawyer's office, they took turns guessing why Kasey had been invited for the reading of Olive's will.

"It could only mean that you're mentioned in it," said Dad as he turned onto the highway toward town.

"But Olive had no material possessions that we know of," said Mom. "She lived in a little room at Shady Oaks for years. She didn't even have her own furniture, did she, Kasey?"

"I don't think so. If she did, she didn't take it with her when she moved in with her sister. She had only a few personal possessions—family photographs and mementos."

"Well, maybe she wanted to leave you some keepsake for sentimental reasons," said Dad.

"Whatever it is," said Mom, "it was thoughtful of her to remember you, honey."

"I think so too, Mom. Whatever it is—if she did leave me something—I'll treasure it forever."

A few minutes later, Dad pulled into the parking lot behind the lawyer's office. As soon as Kasey and her parents entered the little lobby, they were ushered into Mr. Jenkins's office. A stout, bald-headed man with a tiny mustache, he stepped forward and shook their hands firmly. "Come in and sit down. You already know Miss Golden, I presume."

Kasey looked over at Bessie sitting in a large leather chair. She was wearing her best silk flowered dress and had her gray-streaked hair freshly permed.

"You look beautiful, Bessie," said Kasey, sitting down in the leather chair beside her.

"And you look lovely too, dear girl," said Bessie, giving her a little pat on the knee.

"I don't even know why I'm here," Kasey whispered.

Bessie smiled. "You'll find out soon enough, child."

Mr. Jenkins sat down behind his wide desk and cleared his throat as if symbolically calling the meeting to order. "Very well, we are all here. I'll get right to the point." He shuffled several papers on his desk. "As Olive Solomon's attorney, I have called you together for the reading of her will. It's fairly simple and straightforward. Miss Solomon had no heirs except her sister, Bessie Golden, to whom she has bequeathed whatever material possessions she owned at the time of her death."

He paused for a long moment, then said, "Mrs. Solomon had an investment portfolio containing several stocks that have done well in recent days—better, I believe, than even she was aware of. Mrs. Solomon has decreed that this money be set aside in a trust fund for the education of Miss Kassandra Carlone."

Kasey looked around quizzically. "What does this mean? I don't understand."

Bessie reached over and squeezed Kasey's hand. Her eyes gleamed. "It means, dear girl, that you are going to Juilliard after all."

Kasey stared wide-eyed at Mr. Jenkins. "Is that what you're saying? Olive left me her money for college?"

"Yes, Miss Carlone, that's exactly what I'm saying."

"But what about Bessie? Bessie's her sister. She should have Olive's money."

"Goodness, no," scoffed Bessie. "I have all the money an old woman needs, and I have no heirs. Olive and I agreed that you belong at Juilliard, Kasey, and if her money can make that happen . . ."

Tears welled in Kasey's eyes. She looked at her parents. "I don't know what to say."

"Neither do we, honey," said Mom, about to cry.

"Are you sure about this?" asked Dad. "There's no mistake?"

"No mistake," said Mr. Jenkins.

"But wait," said Kasey, suddenly alarmed. "I—I can't go to Juilliard. I already withdrew my application. It's too late to apply for next year."

Her mother spoke up, smiling mysteriously. "No, there's no problem, Kasey. You're still enrolled at Juilliard for next fall."

"But how? I wrote them—"

"I know. But I never mailed the letter. I just felt that somehow it would all work out for you to go."

"You mean, I'm still enrolled?"

"That's right, honey. You gave me the letter to mail, but I put it in my bureau drawer. I hope you understand."

"Understand? Mom, you're terrific!"

"There's one more thing," said Mr. Jenkins. He picked up a sheet of rose-colored stationery and handed it to Bessie. "Mrs. Solomon wrote Miss Carlone a letter when she revised her will a few weeks ago. Miss Golden would like to read her sister's letter to you, Kasey."

Bessie took the letter and began to read with an accent reminiscent of Olive. "My dear Kasey, you were made to scale the heights, to live life to its fullest, to claim the highest prize as your own. Do not be satisfied to walk on shallow ground or be content with the commonplace when, with God's help and your best effort, you can have it all—all that God created you to be, for His glory. If my dusty old money can help you achieve your dearest dreams, then I will die happy. Since you, dear child, introduced me to life's greatest gift, allow me the privilege of helping you share your own extraordinary gift with the world. It is an awesome responsibility to be the best you can be, but I know you have it in you to meet the challenge. Go with God, my dear little one. And know that a stubborn, cantankerous old lady loved you as if you were her own."

17

All the way home Kasey's mother bubbled over with plans. "We'll have to take you shopping, Kasey. You'll need a more sophisticated wardrobe for New York City. Some nice dresses. Comfortable but elegant. I saw some last week at Jacobson's made of cotton poplin. Beautiful colors. Turquoise, fuchsia, magenta. Maybe one of those new tank-style dresses with a bolero jacket. And shoes. You'll need lots of walking shoes. And a warmer coat. What do you think, Tony? Are the winters colder in New York than Springfield?"

"Mom, wait," said Kasey. "My head is spinning. I can't think about clothes and shoes and coats right now. I can't even believe I'm really going to Juilliard!"

"Well, this trust fund does put a whole new slant on things," said Dad. "We'll have to find out when your tuition has to be paid. And we'll need to discuss whether you're going to live in the residence hall or an apartment—"

"Oh, there's no question," said Mom. "I want Kasey living in the residence hall, not some lonely apartment somewhere. She should be with other students. After all, this will be her first time living away from home—"

"Mom," said Kasey, "first-time college students at Juilliard have to live in the residence hall."

"Well, see, Tony? It's settled. She'll be in the residence hall."

"You'll like it, Kasey," said Dad as he pulled into their driveway. "You'll make lots of friends and get a taste of being on your own."

"And you'll come home for Christmas, of course," said Mom. They got out of the car and headed up the porch steps. "Or maybe we could visit you there. I've always wanted to see New York."

"Let's hold off any trips to New York until she graduates," said Dad, opening the front door. "Remember, Kasey might be in the chips, but we're not."

They went inside, and Kasey tossed her purse on the sofa. "I can't believe this," she exclaimed. "You guys already have me graduating, and I just found out an hour ago that I can afford to go to Juilliard."

Her mother gave her a quick hug. "We're just so happy for you. We know this has been your lifelong dream, and now it's finally going to be a reality."

Kasey turned and ran for the stairs. "Don't be happy for me!" she cried, her voice shrill. "I don't even know if I *want* to go to Juilliard!" She dashed into her room, slammed the door, and curled up on her bed with her Pooh Bear. Hot tears spilled onto her cheeks. "Why does everything have to keep changing," she whispered. "Why can't things stay the same until I catch up, until I know what to do!"

There was a knock at her door and her mother's voice: "Kasey, may I talk with you?"

Kasey sat up cross-legged on her bed. "Come in, Mom."

Her mother entered and sat down at the foot of the bed. "Are you OK, honey?"

Kasey nodded. "I'm sorry I yelled. I don't even know why I said such a stupid thing."

"You mean about not being sure about Juilliard? Know what, Kasey? I think you were being honest about your feelings. And I think you need to talk to me, tell me more about how you're feeling right now."

Kasey ran her hand over Pooh Bear's fur. "I don't know how I feel, Mom. That's the problem. All my life I've been so sure about what I wanted to do, what I wanted to be, even where I wanted to go to school. Now that it's all about to happen, I'm petrified. Like I can't move. I can't even think straight." She looked urgently at her mother. "Am I going crazy?"

"No, of course not." Her mother reached over and rubbed Kasey's shoulder. "It's all part of growing up, making choices. When you were little, your choices were simple—what toy you wanted for Christmas, who you wanted to play with, what you wanted for dessert. Now the choices are big ones—where to go to college, who to marry, what to do with the rest of your life. The choices you make now will determine your entire future. I'd say you were foolish if you weren't a little scared."

Kasey was silent a minute, mulling over her mother's words. "But it's more than being scared, Mom. I'm so confused about everything. One minute I want to study at Juilliard so much I can taste it, and the next minute I feel panicky just thinking of leaving home and being separated from everyone I love."

"We'll all be here for you. You know that."

"I know, Mom. But in a week I'm going to graduate, and I feel as if everything stable in my life has been knocked out from under me. I feel—I don't know—shaken to the core, uprooted, buffeted by terrible winds of change. Why do I feel this way?"

Her mother smiled. "I felt that way when I was your age. And look at me—I survived. It'll work out. Trust me. Better yet, trust the Lord. I know He'll see you through this."

"Sure, Mom. I should be shouting for joy that my financial problems are over and I can go to the school of my choice, but—"

"But what? Go on, Kasey. Put it into words. Bring it all out into the open, whatever you feel. Your feelings aren't wrong, honey. They just are. Recognize them, confront them, deal with them honestly."

"But what if—what if it means not going to Juilliard?" Kasey asked haltingly.

"Is that it? Are you afraid of disappointing your dad and me? Are you afraid you won't measure up?"

Kasey pulled at the tuft on Pooh Bear's ear. In a small, anxious voice she asked, "What if I'm not the super talented person Olive Solomon thought I was?"

Her mother stared at her. "What are you saying?"

Hot, bitter tears escaped again. "Mom, I'm only me, a plain, ordinary girl with a knack for playing the piano. How can I match Olive Solomon's expectations of me? How can I ever feel justified taking her hard-earned money? What if I go to Juilliard and end up being just a mediocre pianist? Mom—what if I fail?"

Her mother held her the way she had years ago when Kasey was a child. As deep sobs shook Kasey's frame, her mother soothed, "Go ahead, honey. Cry it out. Get it all out." They sat that way for several minutes, rocking together until Kasey's tears were spent.

Finally her mother said, "Remember when you were a little girl and fell down and skinned your knee? You'd come running to me for a Band-Aid and a kiss. Only now,

I can't fix it with a bandage and a kiss. I can't tell you what's right for you, Kasey. I can't tell you what choices to make for the rest of your life. All I can do is pray that you'll have a heart for God that will be open to His choices."

"I know, Mom," said Kasey, wiping her eyes. "I don't expect you to make my decisions for me. But I sure need your prayers."

"Well, if we can't help you now, your heavenly Father can. If you ask Him to guide you, He will. I know He will. In His own time."

Kasey managed a little smile. "I know it. But sometimes it's hard waiting for His time. I want all the answers now."

"Well, some things you know for sure. You have a wedding to attend in a few days. And after that, a graduation to participate in. In fact, haven't they asked you to play for your graduation ceremony?"

Kasey nodded. "I'll be playing Beethoven's *Appassionata*."

"Well, see? That's settled. That's something you know you're supposed to do."

"But that's just next week. I'm talking about all the weeks and years ahead."

"But don't you see? For God, it may be enough that you know what you're to do today and tomorrow and next week. If you're faithful in those things, He'll open the right doors to your future."

"But would you and Dad be disappointed if I didn't go to Juilliard?"

Her mother was silent a moment. "Whatever you decide, Kasey, we'll stand by you, whether you choose college or marriage, a family or a career, or both! Or whether you stay home or move away. We just want God's best for you, whatever it is."

Kasey stood up and walked over to her window. She gazed out at the darkening sky. "Right now, I don't know, Mom. But I do have one request."

"Of course. What is it?"

"Don't tell anyone about the trust fund Olive left me. Especially not Ryan. Not yet. I'm not sure I can accept it, and until I'm sure, I don't want anyone to know."

Her mother came over and patted her arm. "It's your secret, Kasey, until you're ready to share it."

18

Early Saturday morning, as a pale orange sun peeked over the horizon, Kasey and Ryan began their drive to Middleton for Dusty and Diana's wedding. Kasey's mind was still fuzzy from sleep, and her stomach felt queasy. She wasn't ready to face this day, for many reasons, but she felt too sluggish to think about them now. So she stared out the window at the passing scenery and let her mind go blank.

But Ryan, who was obviously a morning person, kept up a flow of nonstop conversation. "Well, today's the big day," he mused finally. "Dusty walks the plank."

"What's that supposed to mean?"

"Just kidding." He looked curiously at her. "I wouldn't be blathering on like this if you'd say something—anything."

"Really, Ryan, I'm too tired to prattle on about nothing just for the sake of talking."

He shot her a doubtful glance. "Is that what we've

come to in our relationship—trying to think of something to talk about?"

"No, I'm sorry. I'm just—preoccupied."

"You've been that way for days. Is it Dusty? Are you upset about him getting married?"

"No, that's not it at all."

"Then what? Is it us? Something I've done?"

"No, everything's fine. Please, Ryan, don't keep pushing."

"OK, you win. Forget I said anything. We'll start fresh, OK?" He swung his arm around her shoulder and pulled her against him.

She pulled back.

He frowned. "What's wrong?"

"Nothing. How can you drive with just one arm?"

"You never questioned it before."

"But we're on the open highway, going fast."

"It's OK. I'm in control—of the car anyway. But I'm not so sure of this conversation. Are you trying to tell me something?"

"No," she said, too quickly. She lapsed into silence.

He tried again, his voice tender. "Have you been thinking about what we talked about?"

"What?"

"You know. Getting officially engaged at graduation." He squeezed her shoulder. "I probably shouldn't tell you this, but I've been looking at rings."

"Rings? Oh, Ryan, it's too soon. All we've done is talk."

"I know, but I wanted to see what I could afford, and I figure I could charge it on my dad's credit card, then make payments to him. That way I wouldn't have to put the ring on lay-away. You can imagine how long I'd be making payments on lay-away before I could put the ring on your finger. But this way, I might even be able to pick it up by graduation, and—"

"Oh, Ryan!" she lamented.

"What's wrong?"

"You want to give me a ring at graduation? How could you even think of a ring right now?"

"OK, I wasn't going to tell you. I figured it'd be cool surprising you. But if you want to wait a while to make things official, I could put the ring on lay-away after all. Whatever you want, Kasey."

Whatever I want? Heaven help me, I don't know what I want!

Kasey turned her gaze out the window and bit hard on her lower lip until she thought she tasted blood. Angry tears pooled in her eyes, but if she blinked, her mascara would run. She hated herself for what she was feeling now—the sudden rage and impatience with poor, innocent Ryan, her beloved Ryan. He had no idea of the quandary she was in, the opposing poles of emotion that were pulling her in two directions at once. He had no way of knowing that Juilliard was beckoning again and that her old, cherished dreams were slowly resurrecting themselves in her heart.

But what of Ryan? *Oh, God, help me to know what to do!* she prayed silently, with sudden desperation. *And please, God, don't let me hurt Ryan!*

"You OK?" he asked, shaking her shoulder a little.

She stared at him. "What? Yes, I'm fine. Why?"

"You feel so tense, and you look like—like a skittish horse ready to buck and run."

She drew in a breath and let it out slowly. "I could use a Coke and some fries or something. I had a doughnut and juice at the crack of dawn, and now my stomach's growling."

"Mine too. How about if we stop at the next Burger King?"

"Great!"

They didn't say much for the rest of the drive, at least not anything of consequence. Kasey was relieved. She couldn't possibly contemplate getting engaged in her present frame of mind. Her emotions were riding the edge today, on the verge of spilling over, but getting teary-eyed and slushy about her feelings was the last thing she needed on Dusty's wedding day.

They arrived at her grandparents' farm just before noon. Grams and Gramps were already in their "fanciest duds," as Gramps called them.

"You youngsters better get right over to the church," he said. "Diana's already telephoned, wondering where you were. They want to get some pictures before the ceremony."

"We'll go right over," said Kasey. "Ryan, do you want to put on your suit here or at the church?"

"I'll change here, but don't worry, I'll hurry. I know you've got to dress at the church."

Fifteen minutes later they pulled into the church parking lot, and Kasey hurried inside with her cosmetics case. She went directly to the dressing room and burst inside, only to find the most incredible sight. Diana stood in the middle of the room in her wedding gown, looking as if she had just stepped out of *Brides* magazine. She was surrounded by her attendants in their bridesmaid's gowns, putting finishing touches on their makeup and hair. When they saw Kasey, they all greeted her at once.

"Welcome, Kasey, your dress is ready."

"Hurry, Kasey, the photographer is waiting!"

"This way, Kasey, I'll help you into your gown!"

The next few hours were as heady and lively, as filled with euphoria and confusion, laughter and tears, as any

Kasey had ever known. The wedding went off without a hitch. Kasey held her breath and tried to keep her knees from knocking as she marched down the aisle. Walking the aisle in time to the "Wedding March" struck her with a peculiar sensation. She imagined herself the bride and Ryan waiting for her at the altar. And then she analyzed the feelings such a vision prompted. Did the idea strike terror in her heart, or yearning? How did she really feel about the idea of marriage? Marriage to her dear Ryan?

Before she could reach any significant conclusions, she had arrived at the altar and all eyes were turning to Diana as she began her measured strides down the aisle on her father's arm.

Kasey glanced over at Dusty and winced momentarily when she realized that he had eyes for Diana alone. But then, that was as it should be. Dusty was only a friend. Yes, forever a friend.

But Ryan—what about Ryan? As Diana continued her march toward the altar, Kasey scanned the congregation for Ryan. Yes, there he was, and his eyes were on her, not Diana. He smiled slowly and winked, a special glance for her alone.

After the ceremony, Kasey remained with the wedding party while the photographer had his field day, snapping pictures from every possible angle. And just when she thought she was too exhausted to stand any longer on three-inch heels, she had to join the bride and groom in the receiving line to greet the guests.

It was another hour before Kasey could escape to Ryan's side and collapse into a chair while he brought her cake and punch.

"You were beautiful up there," he whispered, kissing her cheek. "I imagined you being my bride at our wedding."

She didn't tell him that she had envisioned the same thing, for different reasons. She only said, "Thanks for the cake and punch. I'm famished."

When it was time for Diana to throw her bridal bouquet, the unmarried girls swarmed around her, arms raised in giddy expectation. Only Kasey held back, until Ryan pushed her forward, urging, "Go out there and catch it for us. Maybe we'll be next!"

Reluctantly she joined the others, remaining at the edge of the crowd with her arms barely raised, but sure enough, Diana—her best friend since kindergarten—spotted her and aimed the bouquet intentionally in her direction. Kasey groaned as the fragrant, pale pink flowers fell easily into her hands. The other girls growled and complained and gradually dispersed, leaving Kasey alone staring at the bouquet and contemplating what it all meant.

Ryan dashed up to her and swung her up in his arms. "It's a sign, Kasey," he declared. "It means you'll be the next bride!"

"No," she said thickly. "It doesn't mean anything at all. It could be a—a bouquet of good-byes! That's all I've collected lately. First Dusty, and then Olive, and next it'll be—" She stopped in horror as she realized what she was saying.

Ryan picked up on it too. He stared squint-eyed at her. "And next it'll be—who, Kasey? Who were you going to say? Me? Next it'll be me?"

"No! No one. Nothing. It's just an expression."

He took her arm and held her fast. "I don't think so. I think you've been trying to tell me something for days. What is it?"

"Not here, Ryan," she said, realizing they were attracting attention. "Later, when we're alone, OK?"

It was nearly dusk when the wedding couple scrambled to their car amid a shower of rice and a clatter of tin cans. The warm June air rang with shouts and laughter. The fragrance of roses and the aura of romance mingled in the breeze. Kasey felt the sweet exhilaration of the moment, a delirious light-headedness, the tempting tension of unexpressed passion. This was a night to be in love with love.

After the bride and groom had squealed off past a sea of waving hands, Ryan and Kasey bade their friends good night, and Ryan walked her to the car, his arm circling her waist. Kasey noted that he looked more than handsome in his crisp dark suit, his hair slightly tousled, the spicy scent of his aftershave mingling with his warm peppermint breath. Before opening the car door, he drew Kasey into his arms and kissed her with unexpected yearning. Caught off guard, Kasey yielded to the kiss and found herself kissing him back. For an instant, it was as if she and Ryan were the bride and groom who had just dashed from the church. And now it was time for the honeymoon.

But no. Wait. Kasey drew back and shook her head, her mind whirling. "We've got to talk, Ryan," she managed weakly.

He opened the car door, and she stepped inside. He went around and got in too and stuck the key in the ignition. "Where?"

"Where? Where what?" she asked, confused.

"Where do you want to talk? Here? At the farm? Back in Springfield?"

"Grams and Gramps are expecting us to stay there tonight."

"But where can we be alone? I have a feeling this is going to be heavy duty."

"Right here? In the church parking lot?"

"OK." He turned off the ignition. "What's up?"

Haltingly she told him about the meeting at the lawyer's office and the reading of Olive Solomon's will. She concluded with the astonishing news that she was certain would have Ryan up in arms. "Olive left me a trust fund to pay for my college education, Ryan. That means I have the money I need for Juilliard."

His expression registered incredulity, then shock, and finally dismay. "Juilliard? I thought you'd given up that idea."

"I had to, because I had no money."

"I thought it was because of us too. I thought you wanted to stay in Springfield and go to the community college with me."

"I did, Ryan, but—"

"But now it's not your only option, right? Now you've got Juilliard in your pocket. That's where you're going next year, isn't it?"

Kasey sat very still, staring out at the darkening sky. In a very small voice she said, "Yes, Ryan. I'm going to Juilliard."

"So how long ago did you decide that? And when were you going to get around to telling me?"

She looked earnestly at him. "I hadn't decided. I didn't know what I was going to do—until this moment. It's true. This very moment I realized it. I've been given a chance, Ryan, an incredible opportunity. It's a miracle, and I can't turn my back on it. I've got to follow my dream."

"What about our dream of being together? Getting engaged? What happens to us when you traipse off to New York?"

She hated the wounded sound in his voice, the deep, searing disappointment. Why did the fulfillment of one person's dream mean the death of another's?

"I didn't want to hurt you, Ryan," she said unevenly. "I love you. I really do."

His tone was clipped, resentful. "But not enough, right?"

"I don't know. Honestly, I don't. Maybe someday we can be together. I want that. I really do. But first—first I've got to risk something, risk failure, risk the unknown. It's not enough for me to be protected and cared for, Ryan. I've got to give God and the world everything that's inside me—the talent, the passions, the dreams. I've got to see what I can become, what God can accomplish through me. Can you understand that?"

He nodded grudgingly. "You wouldn't be my Kasey if you didn't feel that way."

She searched his eyes in the darkness. "Does that mean you really do understand?"

"I understand, but I don't like it." He heaved a disgruntled sigh. "I suppose next you'll say you want to break up."

She was silent a moment, then said softly, "No, I don't want that. I hope what we share, the feelings we have for each other, will stand the test of time—and distance. I hope, after we've both had time to change and grow and become whoever we're supposed to be—I hope then you'll come to me with a ring, Ryan, and ask me to spend my life with you."

"And what will you say if I ask that question?"

"I hope I'll say I've waited all my life for you and I never want us to be apart again."

Ryan pulled Kasey over against him, into the crook of his arm, and pressed her head against his cheek. She could feel his tears washing her face and feel the silent sobs in his chest. Her own tears fell freely, but they weren't tears of anguish. There was something cleansing and liberating in these tears. In fact, a sense of peace and joy welled in her chest, rising like a geyser of exultation. It was the sort of feeling she had when she knew she was making the choices God wanted her to make, no matter how difficult or impossible they seemed.

"I'll never stop loving you, Kasey," Ryan whispered. "And I'll never stop believing you're the girl for me."

"I'll always love you too, Ryan," she answered, "and I pray I'm the girl God picked for you. No matter what happens I'll never forget you."

He kissed her face, her hair. "And no matter how long we're apart, Kase, I'll never say good-bye."

For a while they were silent, savoring their closeness in the muggy car. Kasey loved being in Ryan's arms, feeling safe and cherished. It was one of the absolute best feelings in the world.

But first, there were other worlds to conquer. God had already opened the door, and He would prepare the way. She could trust Him for that. She could trust Him with her life. And she would!

In the stillness of the automobile, surrounded by the cocoon warmth of Ryan's arms, Kasey thought ahead to her high school graduation. In just three days she would be walking across the stage at Springfield High to claim her diploma. And she would sit at the grand piano on center stage and play a Beethoven sonata for a vast audience of parents and students.

Already she could feel her pulse quicken and her heart pound, but she knew God would quell her terror and help her to play her best. And as long as she was willing to become what God had created her to be, she could not possibly fail.

Unexpectedly, she remembered the words Olive Solomon had written to her in her final letter: *Kasey, my dear girl, you were made to scale the heights, to live life to its fullest, to claim the highest prize as your own. . . . It is an awesome responsibility to be the best you can be, but I know you have it in you to meet the challenge.*

Silently Kasey prayed, *Please, God, let it be so!*

After a while, she tilted her face up to Ryan's and said, "Maybe we should head back to the farm. Grams and Gramps will be wondering where we are."

Ryan nodded. "OK, but I'm not sure we've resolved anything."

"We have," she assured him. "We're going to be OK. I've got this feeling." She reached over on the seat for Diana's bridal bouquet and breathed in the fragrance of the petals.

"Ryan, did I ever tell you what Bessie said about the daisies?"

"Daisies?"

"Olive's daisies. At the funeral. Bessie said it wasn't just a bouquet of good-byes. She was right." Kasey plucked a rose and handed it to Ryan. "I promise. It's also a bouquet of hellos. A bouquet of new beginnings."

Moody Press, a ministry of the Moody Bible Institute,
is designed for education, evangelization, and edification.
If we may assist you in knowing more about Christ
and the Christian life, please write us without obligation:
Moody Press, c/o MLM, Chicago, Illinois 60610.